THE RED DEVIL
BATTERY SIGN

By TENNESSEE WILLIAMS

PLAYS

Baby Doll (a screenplay)
Camino Real
Cat on a Hot Tin Roof
Clothes for a Summer Hotel
Dragon Country
The Glass Menagerie
A Lovely Sunday for Creve Coeur
The Red Devil Battery Sign
Small Craft Warnings
Stopped Rocking and Other Screenplays
A Streetcar Named Desire
Sweet Bird of Youth
THE THEATRE OF TENNESSEE WILLIAMS, VOLUME I
Battle of Angels, A Streetcar Named Desire, The Glass Menagerie
THE THEATRE OF TENNESSEE WILLIAMS, VOLUME II
The Eccentricities of a Nightingale, Summer and Smoke, The Rose Tattoo, Camino Real
THE THEATRE OF TENNESSEE WILLIAMS, VOLUME III
Cat on a Hot Tin Roof, Orpheus Descending, Suddenly Last Summer
THE THEATRE OF TENNESSEE WILLIAMS, VOLUME IV
Sweet Bird of Youth, Period of Adjustment, The Night of the Iguana
THE THEATRE OF TENNESSEE WILLIAMS, VOLUME V
The Milk Train Doesn't Stop Here Anymore, Kingdom of Earth (The Seven Descents of Myrtle), Small Craft Warnings, The Two-Character Play
THE THEATRE OF TENNESSEE WILLIAMS, VOLUME VI
27 Wagons Full of Cotton and Other Short Plays
THE THEATRE OF TENNESSEE WILLIAMS, VOLUME VII
In the Bar of a Tokyo Hotel and Other Plays
27 Wagons Full of Cotton and Other Plays
The Two-Character Play
Vieux Carré

POETRY

Androgyne, Mon Amour
In the Winter of Cities

PROSE

Collected Stories
Eight Mortal Ladies Possessed
Hard Candy and Other Stories
The Knightly Quest and Other Stories
One Arm and Other Stories
The Roman Spring of Mrs. Stone
Where I Live: Selected Essays

TENNESSEE WILLIAMS

THE RED DEVIL BATTERY SIGN

A NEW DIRECTIONS BOOK

Manufactured in the United States of America

First published clothbound and as New Directions
Paperbook 650 in 1988

Published simultaneously in Canada by
Penguin Books Canada Limited

Library of Congress Cataloging-in-Publication Data

Williams, Tennessee, 1911-1983
The red devil battery sign.
(A New Directions Book)
I. Title.
PS3545.I5365R3   1988   812'.54   87-15212
ISBN 0-8112-1046-4
ISBN 0-8112-1047-2 (pbk.)

New Directions Books are published for James Laughlin
by New Directions Publishing Corporation,
80 Eighth Avenue, New York 10011

TO KEITH BAXTER

THE RED DEVIL
BATTERY SIGN

The Red Devil Battery Sign was presented by Gene Persson for Ruby Productions Limited at the Round House, London, on June 8, 1977, and at the Phoenix Theatre, London, on July 7, 1977. It was directed by Keith Baxter and David Leland; it was designed by Bob Ringwood and Kate Owen; lighting and projections were by David Hersey; and original music was by Mario Ramos. The cast, in order of appearance, was as follows:

WOLF	KEN SHORTER
GRIFFIN	MICHAEL ENSIGN
CHARLIE	GARRY MCDERMOTT
FIRST DRUNK	GLENN WILLIAMS
SECOND DRUNK	DON STAITON
HOTEL GUEST	SIMON WALSH
HOOKER	DEBORAH BENZIMRA
WOMAN DOWNTOWN	ESTELLE KOHLER
MARIACHIS	MARIO RAMOS, ALEJANDRO VASQUEZ, ALFONSO SALAZAR, PETER LUKAS
CREWCUT	PETER LUKAS
KING	KEITH BAXTER
PERLA	MARIA BRITNEVA
McCABE	PIERCE BROSNAN
LA NIÑA	NITZA SAUL
JUDGE COLLISTER	ROBERT HENDERSON
FIRST CONVENTIONEER	SIMON WALSH
SECOND CONVENTIONEER	GLENN WILLIAMS
DRUMMER	RAAD RAWI
PHARMACIST	ROBERT HENDERSON
WASTELAND BOYS	TONY GARNER, TONY LONDON, KELVIN OMARD, ELVIS PAYNE, MARIO RENZULLO, DON STAITON, SIMON WALSH

This edition of *The Red Devil Battery Sign* is based on a 1979 revision, by the author, of the text used for the London production. The play now includes the following characters (in order of appearance):

GRIFFIN
HOOKER
DRUNK
WOMAN DOWNTOWN
CHARLIE
KING
THREE MARIACHIS
JULIO (the oldest Mariachi)
CREWCUT
PERLA
LA NIÑA
McCABE
FIRST CONVENTIONEER
SECOND CONVENTIONEER
DRUMMER
OLD MAN (the Pharmacist)
CAB DRIVER (offstage)
WOLF
BOY
OTHER WASTELAND BOYS

ACT ONE

||||||||||||||||||||||||||||||||||||||||||||||||||||||||||||||||||||||||||||||||||||||||||||||||||||||||||||||||||||||||

SCENE ONE

||||||||||||||||||||||||||||||||||||||||||||||||||||||||||||||||||||||||||||||||||||||||||||||||||||||||||||||||||||||||

The cocktail lounge of the Yellow Rose Hotel in downtown Dallas. At curtain-rise, only the bar is hotly lighted. A small group of Mariachis play softly. A Drunk is talking to Charlie, the barman. At a slight distance, the hotel manager, Mr. Griffin, is looking on with disapproval. A restless Hooker crosses to a bar stool adjoining the Drunk's.

||||||||||||||||||||||||||||||||||||||||||||||||||||||||||||||||||||||||||||||||||||||||||||||||||||||||||||||||||||||||

GRIFFIN: I'm sorry, Miss, but unescorted ladies aren't allowed at the bar.

HOOKER [*in a broad Texas drawl*]: What makes you think I'm unescawted, huh? [*She nudges the Drunk, who pivots to inspect her, and speaks to him.*] He calls me not escawted. [*She digs an elbow lower into the Drunk's paunch.*]

DRUNK: This young lady's escawted, personally by me.

[*The Woman Downtown enters the upstage perimeter of the lighted area. She is tall, with a pale, exquisitely molded face: an immediately striking elegance of presence. She has a light coat (loose-woven cloth of gold) thrown over her dress. She stands by a rear table and surveys the lounge as if she suspected some menacing element in it.*]

GRIFFIN [*to Drunk*]: Are you registered *here?*

DRUNK: Here's my room-key, here.

[*The Drunk digs into a pants' pocket and empties an avalanche of coins and crumpled bills on the floor.*]

1

HOOKER: Aw!

[*She stoops immediately to collect the bills, returning some to the Drunk and slipping others into her bag. The Woman Downtown laughs wryly, softly. She removes the light coat and reveals a stunning iridescent Oriental sheath with a delicate dragon design on it.*]

DRUNK: And here's my bus'ness card. See what firm I'm with? To check out this hotel as possible headquarters for our next month convention?

GRIFFIN [*abruptly, very impressed*]: —Thank you, sir. Charlie, offer this young couple drinks on the house, excuse me. [*He crosses to the Woman Downtown. A blond Crewcut enters.*] Well! Good evening, Ma'am.

WOMAN DOWNTOWN [*icily*]: Good evening, Mr.—

GRIFFIN: Griffin. —I was surprised to see you down here.

WOMAN DOWNTOWN: Why? What surprised you about it?

GRIFFIN: When you were checked in here by Judge Collister.

WOMAN DOWNTOWN: When I checked in was when?

GRIFFIN: I'd have to check the books to give you the exact night—

WOMAN DOWNTOWN: The approximate night, a week ago, two weeks, since the last ice age?

GRIFFIN: What I do remember clearly right now is that Judge Collister said that you were to have complete anonymity here and complete rest and seclusion.

2

WOMAN DOWNTOWN: Oh, rest and seclusion I've had a massive dose of. Only morning visits from a doctor who *said* he'd been told to visit me by the *Judge.*

GRIFFIN [*repeatedly, nervously*]: Yes. Fine. I see. Hmmm.

WOMAN DOWNTOWN [*overlapping*]: —At first the injections were agreeably sedative, then not so agreeably, then not agreeably at all since I found myself falling to the floor when I got out of bed. [*She gets progressively louder.*] Then I stopped letting him in, locked and bolted the door against him when he knocked.

GRIFFIN: You're being overheard by strangers at the bar. You don't want attention in the public rooms. You see, I regard your anonymity here more highly than you, Ma'am. With such a distinguished person we—

WOMAN DOWNTOWN: You give yourself away.

GRIFFIN: I haven't spoken your name.

WOMAN DOWNTOWN: You refer to me as "a distinguished person."

GRIFFIN: There's something so apparent about you.

WOMAN DOWNTOWN [*cutting through contemptuously*]: I came in here covered from *head* to *foot* by the Judge's car-blanket and *said* and *did* nothing . . . stayed speechless in a wheelchair while the Judge said that I must have anonymity here and paid you exceptionally well for providing it for me. But since you've penetrated that anonymity—I am ready to check out, my luggage is packed. I want to get word to my guardian, Judge Collister, to come here for me at once. I've made continual efforts to reach the Judge by phone. For some reason I'm not able to make outside calls from my suite; the calls are not completed. I've complained to the operator; still they're not *completed.*

GRIFFIN: You are raising your voice, Ma'am. I don't think you realize that your face is recognizable—

WOMAN DOWNTOWN [*putting on dark glasses*]: There he is, the blond Crewcut. *He* certainly *recognizes* me! Whenever I enter the corridor, he starts to follow a couple of paces behind me, and I retreat to my rest and seclusion.

GRIFFIN: That young man is our house detective, Ma'am.

WOMAN DOWNTOWN: Oh, your house dick. What is he trailing me for, of what does he *suspect* me? Call him over, tell him I'd like to *know.*

GRIFFIN: He has to stay by the door. Undesirables try to enter, you know. My wife had a sister who spent a few months at Paradise Meadows Nursing Home. She had some treatments there called electric shock.

WOMAN DOWNTOWN: Shock, yes, electric.

GRIFFIN: The treatments were highly effective in the case I mentioned—

WOMAN DOWNTOWN: Brainwashed. . . . Well, I am not. My foster father the Judge maneuvered my escape from Paradise Meadows after five days of their marvelous treatment.

GRIFFIN: Now, as to the Judge, you would naturally be unable to call him at his residence or office. —Would you allow me to order you a drink? Brandy? Charlie, the lady would like some brandy.

WOMAN DOWNTOWN: No she would *not.* A glass of champagne *laced* with a little brandy; I need to keep a clear head in this atmosphere of intrigue here. —What about Judge Collister?

GRIFFIN: Just have your drink first, before we—hmmm . . .

[*Charlie serves the drink; she drains it immediately.*]

WOMAN DOWNTOWN: I said laced with, not loaded. Now what have you to tell me?

GRIFFIN: That grand old man has been on the critical list at the New Medical Center since later on the night he delivered you here, Ma'am.

WOMAN DOWNTOWN: Christ, on the—critical—which night? —He brought me here—and you haven't informed me? I want a car, a rental limousine. [*She has caught hold of his jacket.*]

GRIFFIN: If you'll let go of my jacket, I will call the limousine service. [*He glances away, picks up the bar phone, glancing back at her, nodding, smiling—a grimace.*] Car for the lady at the bar.

WOMAN DOWNTOWN: Perhaps you'd like the button I tore off your jacket.

[*Griffin leaves. The subdued talk among the men at the bar is brought up.*]

DRUNK: Any goddam kid won't register for draft is a traitor to—

CHARLIE: Yestuhday, f'rinstance, Nation'l Guard tried to round up those kids that live in the Hollow, west a city, register 'em. I tell yuh they couldn't get near 'em, blown up two squad cars with bottles of nitro!

DRUNK: Savages in city. Oughta go in there with flame throwers, burn 'em outa their dug-outs like we done gooks in 'Nam.

WOMAN DOWNTOWN: Hear! Hear! It's a patriotic duty for you middle-aged gentlemen over draft age! DO IT! You're not too old to discharge a missile, are you, at— Sorry, did I speak? I'm not supposed to speak!

DRUNK: You spoke distinctly, baby. I'd like t' discharge a missile into . . . [*He completes the lewd remark behind his hand.*]

WOMAN DOWNTOWN [*laughing mockingly*]: That *would* be a little beyond your capacity just now, and if lightning does not strike once, it cannot strike twice.

CHARLIE [*in response to a whisper*]: Bananas.

DRUNK: Aw? Could use a chiquita banana and I don't mean *mañana*. [*He stumbles toward the Woman Downtown.*]

WOMAN DOWNTOWN: Your vision must be blurred. Your wife has retired to the ladies' loo.

DRUNK: That hooker?

WOMAN DOWNTOWN: What a shocking term to use for your *wife*.

DRUNK: Me? Married to a hooker?

WOMAN DOWNTOWN: Some gentlemen do marry above their station.

DRUNK: Nah me, Babe. Here, take this key while I finish my drink. Go up to my room and I promise I won't disappoint yuh!

6

WOMAN DOWNTOWN: *—Hands off!* —I don't want that, I never did want that, all that I ever wanted was—

[*Her face and voice soften. She makes a vague gesture in space. King Del Rey appears. Originally called Rey, this Texan born on the border and with some Spanish-Indian blood in him, later called himself by the English word for "Rey." He has a natural kingliness—an air of authority—about him, with just a hint of that bravado that masks an anxiety that the authority may slip from him. This hint appears only at moments. Now as he stands at stage left, having just entered the revolving door of the "club" lounge, he exaggerates the bravado, the air of command, to something almost macho.*]

MARIACHIS: *¡Hola, King! ¡Hola, amigo!*

[*The band plays "El Rey." There have been jocular greetings in Spanish from the musicians, which King has returned.*]

KING: *Es una noche caliente, ¿eh?*

[*The Woman Downtown appears diverted from her own situation by King's entrance.*]

WOMAN DOWNTOWN: *—Sí, señor, es una noche caliente.*

KING [*impressed by her beauty and style*]: The lady speaks some Spanish?

WOMAN DOWNTOWN: Oh, yes, the lady is a linguist, speaks many tongues.

DRUNK [*at the bar*]: Yeh, that lady's got a tongue in her mouth runnin' outa control.

KING [*to the Drunk*]: You are on my bar stool. Get off it before you're knocked off it.

[*The Drunk stares at King a moment, then shrugs and staggers from the bar.*]

DRUNK: Where's a—man's room? [*He exits.*]

WOMAN DOWNTOWN [*to King*]: Ah, now, seats at the bar, two adjoining. Will you be my escort? An unescorted lady is not allowed at the bar.

KING: *Sí. Con mucho gusto.* Sit down, please. Charlie's opened my beer. Charlie, give the lady a drink.

WOMAN DOWNTOWN: Thank you, but my "special" drink was already provided. Strong drinks aren't good in hot weather, overheat you internally. Even in a cool room, I'm conscious of heat outside. People bring it in the room with them, like—little moons of perspiration under the armpits.

KING [*embarrassed*]: I took a shower and put on clean white shirt just before I come downtown, but the shirt's already stickin' to me. I ain't crowdin' you, am I?

WOMAN DOWNTOWN: Oh, no. Am I crowding you? I find it hard to keep a completely vertical position when so tired . . . [*She is leaning against his shoulder; then she removes an atomizer from her evening bag.*] This is a cooling little imported fragrance, *Vol de Nuit,* translates to Night Flight. Everything translates to something when your head's full of tongues, you know.

CHARLIE: Sure you don't want some rest?

WOMAN DOWNTOWN: I am resting comfortably, but I must keep an eye out for that rental limousine.

CHARLIE: How is Pearla, King?

KING: Charlie, it's pronounced "Perla," like in a pear, not "Pearla" like in a pearl.

[*The four Mariachis complete a song. The oldest one calls out to King.*]

JULIO: Come up and do a solo, King.

KING: Is that a test you give me? Okay, challenge—accepted!

[*He rises to join them. The Woman Downtown clutches his arm.*]

WOMAN DOWNTOWN [*in an urgent whisper, glancing fearfully at Crewcut, who has moved by the door*]: Don't leave me, please! Stay with me!

KING: I do a song for you, special! Ha! First performance since San Antone! And without La Niña?

MARIACHI: ¿La Niña *está en* Chicago?

KING: You bet La Niña is burning up Chicago! Is at a spot called The Pump Room—

WOMAN DOWNTOWN [*rising*]: Please! Please! Later! Sing later!

KING [*not understanding her agitation*]: But I sing for you. ¡Hombres, para la señorita! [*He turns to the Woman Downtown.*] ¿Qué canción le gustaría escuchar, señorita? What song you like, lady?

WOMAN DOWNTOWN: Any, any will do!

KING: *Volver.*

[*The Mariachis begin a ranchero: sensual rhythm. King sings solo, his look remaining on the Woman Downtown.*]

CREWCUT: Car for the lady at the bar!

WOMAN DOWNTOWN [*with a desperate, involuntary cry*]: My car!

[*She rushes dizzily toward the exit and stumbles. King rushes to help her to her feet.*]

Thanks, see you don't leave!

[*King remains, bewildered, by the door. Crewcut and Charlie may exchange significant glances or signs. After a few loud moments, she rushes wildly back in.*]

A cab, same cab, same monster grinning at me, I swear! *I demand—*

[*She collapses to her knees. Crewcut stares imperturbably ahead. Charlie lifts the bar phone. King rushes to lift the Woman Downtown.*]

KING [*softly*]: What's the trouble, tell me, what's the trouble!

[*She sobs, unable to speak. King turns to Charlie.*]

She stay in hotel?

CHARLIE: Don't get involved—I call the doctor?

WOMAN DOWNTOWN: Noooo!

KING: Whatcha mean? "Not involved," huh?

CHARLIE: She's mental: under surveillance.

[*Griffin has entered from the lounge.*]

KING: Lady? Lady?

WOMAN DOWNTOWN [*to King*]: Please, help me upstairs, Penthouse B! —I need seclusion and rest . . .

[*King supports her gently offstage.*]

GRIFFIN [*to Crewcut*]: Follow! [*To the Mariachis.*] Music, music!

[*Crewcut follows rapidly upstage and off. The Mariachis resume.*]

THE LOUNGE IS DIMMED OUT

SCENE TWO

The set is a sketchy evocation of the bedroom of Penthouse B, parlor entrance at left.

||||||||||||||||||||||||||||||||||||||||||||||||||||||||||||||||||||||||||||||||||||||||||||||||||||||||||||||||||||||||

WOMAN DOWNTOWN [*to King, still in the parlor*]: I suppose you think I'd gone crazy down there, isn't that what you think?

[*King appears in the doorway; he regards her with a slightly apprehensive reserve.*]

Lock that hall door, bolt it, I think they called their "doctor"! —That elevator hasn't gone down, I haven't heard the elevator door close! Did you notice the young man with close-cropped hair who came all the way up here, carefully ignoring my pretense of being unable to stand unsupported? Would you, while I get some glasses out of the little ice-chest, slip quietly into the corridor and see if he's hanging around still.

KING: Aw, him, he asked my name as we come up here.

WOMAN DOWNTOWN: Didn't give it, did you?

KING: Naw, naw, if a guy has a friendly attitude and he asked my name or he's got some reason to ask like I was witness to a car crash, I'll give my name, but—

WOMAN DOWNTOWN: Quick, please check the corridor for Crewcut who dogs my steps, every step I take outside this Penthouse B! Quickly, quietly. Don't be alarmed, I'm not demented.

[*King sets the chair behind her.*]

KING: *Estate, estate quieta—un momento.*

[*He exits. She waits tensely till he returns.*]

Tienes razón.

WOMAN DOWNTOWN: Out there, was he?

KING: Leanin' against wall, scribbling in a notebook. He snapped it shut when he seen me, give me a hard look and got in the elevator.

WOMAN DOWNTOWN: And at last I hear its descent with him in it, I trust.

KING: So why don't you sit down and catch your breath in this chair?

WOMAN DOWNTOWN [*distractedly*]: Chair?

KING: I put it right here for you.

WOMAN DOWNTOWN: Ah . . . thoughtful, but when I'm disturbed, I have to stay on my feet and keep occupied with—ice bucket, drinks?

KING: Leave that to me, you sit down before you—

WOMAN DOWNTOWN: Fall down?

KING: In that beautiful dress.

WOMAN DOWNTOWN: This iridescent sheath of goldfish color was given me by General Susang's wife. Some tyrants have exquisite tastes in fabrics. The gift has some very unpleasant associations, but you can't blame a gift for the giver's moral corruption and everything else was packed for departure if any means of escape presented itself, refuge in the country estate of my

13

guardian. [*She takes a breath.*] Jailkeeper Griffin downstairs just informed me my guardian's been hospitalized since the night he delivered me here. Shattered what's left of my nerves. God! Did you think I'd flipped out in the lounge?

KING: What I think or don't think, does it matter?

WOMAN DOWNTOWN: Yes. Very much.

KING: Why?

WOMAN DOWNTOWN: You are actually the only person I've encountered at the—Paradise—Rose?—who strikes me as being a person I could appeal to for assistance, now that—

[*She runs out of breath.*]

KING [*pressing gently down on her shoulders to seat her in the chair*]: This hotel. What was that y'called it?

WOMAN DOWNTOWN: I hope you put that word "hotel" in quotes.

KING: In?

WOMAN DOWNTOWN: Quotes—sorry. I keep forgetting your native language is Spanish. You're Mexican, aren't you?

KING: Don't let that scare you. Some people, y'know, they think all Mexicans are criminals like, like rapists, y'know, like—rapists.

WOMAN DOWNTOWN: Ridiculous—misapprehension.

KING: I was born close to the border, but I'm a Texan. —My mother tole me my father was a gringo, but his name was Spanish—Del Rey. —Oh, I brought your coat and bag up.

WOMAN DOWNTOWN: *Gracias.*

KING [*handing the bag to her*]: You better check the bag to make sure the cash is still in it.

WOMAN DOWNTOWN: There was nothing much in it *but* money.

KING: And money means nothing to you.

WOMAN DOWNTOWN: Nothing compared to some documents which I—

[*She stops, uncertain whether she can go into the subject of "documents" even with this charmingly ingenuous man. She thinks that it might be wiser to change the subject till she knows him better.*]

Didn't you say you were going to serve as bartender at the little bar? A Margarita? Or a Tequila Sunrise?

KING: For me—the limit is beer.

WOMAN DOWNTOWN: I think you mean I was loaded in the lounge.

KING: I didn't say you was. I, I—got no—opinion.

WOMAN DOWNTOWN: My drink was loaded, I wasn't.

KING: Y'say your drinks was loaded. By Charlie the barman?

WOMAN DOWNTOWN: Who else mixes drinks down there but Fatso at the bar: Charlie the barman is he? —Let me remove the luggage from the bed. I mean, would you? I'm still in a shocked condition. The news about my guardian, Judge Collister's very

15

suspiciously sudden hospitalization and on the critical list at—
New Meadows—New—Medical—

KING: I got the luggage off. You rest on the bed.

WOMAN DOWNTOWN: Oh Lord, how I do long to! It wouldn't embarrass you if I—you wouldn't misinterpret it as a—provocation?

KING: No, I—don't—take advantage of—ladies . . .

[*His voice is hoarse with conflicting impulses. A Vuitton suitcase falls from his nervous fingers, spilling its contents, delicate lingerie, a leopard-skin coat, an ermine jacket, etc.*]

Perdóname, one arm, one hand, the fingers—still—don't operate right, I—

[*She has gasped and immediately snatched up some photostatic papers among the spilled articles.*]

—specially when I'm— Did, did—anything break?

WOMAN DOWNTOWN: Papers don't break—

[*They have bent together, she for the papers, he for the delicate lingerie. They straighten simultaneously, faces nearly touching. She is searching his eyes and is abruptly convinced of his total honesty. He notices he has picked up a pair of lace panties and drops them like a hot coal. She shrieks with the laughter of released tension.*]

My God, but you Latins do have an instinct for the most intimate bits of apparel!—

KING: Me? No, I'm—I didn't—notice, I—

[*His embarrassment, frustration, and their betrayal, anger him. He takes a suddenly commanding tone.*]

Set back down on the bed!—I put it in the box for you.

WOMAN DOWNTOWN [*suddenly serious, touching his face as you might a child's*]: I shouldn't have laughed. You Latin men don't understand women's laughter.

KING: You think I'm buffoon, *payaso?* A clown?

WOMAN DOWNTOWN: Oh, please no. It was a release of tension. *¿Comprende?* I realized all at once that I could trust you completely. [*There is a "moment" between them.*] —May I, just to make up?

[*She gives him a quick, light kiss. Clearly she has now decided that intimacy will secure him as a confederate.*]

KING: Why don't you just stay on the bed?

WOMAN DOWNTOWN: I'd fall asleep and who knows what I'd dream? Of my previous confinement, of that butcher's block of a bed with straps that tore my skin till I screamed—before the electric shock and the Judge saved me from them. Oh, they would have continued the shock treatments till they killed me, wouldn't have stopped short of assassination to discover who held the original copies of those documents. You see, my memory's still scrambled like—eggs ranchero . . .

KING: —*Huevos rancheros,* huh?

WOMAN DOWNTOWN: That's right, *hombre.* Exactly like *huevos rancheros*, good for breakfast, but not for—recollection . . .

KING: I like 'em for a late supper when I can't sleep, yeah, with pepper sauce, tabasco.

17

WOMAN DOWNTOWN: Oh, you like that, do you? I have McIlhenny's tabasco on my little bar here. Why don't you call room service and ask for two orders of *huevos rancheros?* Room service is the one thing that I can always get on that phone.

KING: You—serious?

[*He is now crouched by the bed, folding the delicate lingerie very neatly and tenderly into the suitcase. There is a knock at the door. She catches her breath softly.*]

WOMAN DOWNTOWN [*in a whisper*]: Must be their doctor. Did you bolt the door?

[*He nods.*]

Call through it and tell them I won't see him. Don't, don't admit that impostor!

[*King crosses rapidly out.*]

KING [*offstage*]: The lady is all right now, don't need to see you. [*There is the sound of muffled protest.*] I told you she won't see you, so get lost!

[*He returns.*]

WOMAN DOWNTOWN: Thank you—oh God, thank you.

KING: *Por nada. —Recógete en tu cama. No hay peligro conmigo—* There is no danger with me. Now I call room service.

[*She sinks, sobbing voluptuously, onto the bed. He lifts the phone, but stares at the woman as she slowly, sensuously writhes on the bed's surface. He is startled.*]

—*Oh, yes, please, room service!*

[*He speaks to the Woman Downtown, hoarsely, through dry lips.*]

Now I am calling room service—they are ringing room service. —Hey Juan, *¿qué tal? Sí ¡Rey! ¡Escucha! Queremos dos platos de huevos rancheros, Chico, para—* What is your name, Miss?

[*Pause.*]

WOMAN DOWNTOWN [*sitting up slowly to face him*]: That I can't give you. [*She smiles slowly, sadly.*] Call me the Woman Downtown—

KING [*his eyes lingering on her*]: I'll just say for Penthouse B. —*Para* Penthouse B. Ha? *Cierra la boca*—you fink. You wanta tell Perla? You wanta be dead tomorrow?

[*He starts to put down the phone.*]

WOMAN DOWNTOWN: Don't hang up!

KING: Hold on, Juan— You want something else? —To go with the *huevos rancheros?*

[*She stands thinking.*]

WOMAN DOWNTOWN: He's a good friend of yours? One you can trust, even here?

KING: *Sí, sí,* a very good friend from Piedras Negras, Texas— my hometown.

WOMAN DOWNTOWN: —Ask him to put through a call, at once, to the New Medical Center and inquire about the condition of

19

my guardian, Judge Leland Collister, who's hospitalized there—
identify himself as the Judge's cook, they might give him a
report.

KING: Why can't I call from here?

WOMAN DOWNTOWN: The call wouldn't be put through.

KING [*into phone*]: —Juan, *otra cosa, muy discreta, Llama el
hospital—*

WOMAN DOWNTOWN: New Medical Center.

KING: *El Nuevo Centro Medical. Sí.* New Medical Center.
Y pregunta por—

WOMAN DOWNTOWN: Judge *Le*-land *Col*-lis-ter, *su condición.*

KING: Judge Leland Collister, *su condición.* Say you work for
him, cook, *cocinero, tú sabes. ¡Ahora, pronto!*

[*He cradles the phone, his eyes lingering on her. The Woman
Downtown sits tensely at the foot of the bed. He tries to
lighten it up.*]

He says to me, musta been up with room service, he says you're
in the Penthouse with the classy—

WOMAN DOWNTOWN: —Classy what?

KING: Some a these spicks, y'know, they got a—

WOMAN DOWNTOWN: Classy *what?* Papaya? Oh, I am flattered,
you know.

KING: As, some a the, y'know, they got a—*boca grosera* . . .

20

[*He looks away, blushing. Pause. She kicks off her high-heeled slippers and falls onto the edge of the bed. Pause. She spreads her legs slightly.*]

WOMAN DOWNTOWN: —Papaya is the name of a tropical fruit.

KING: —Hmm—yes . . .

WOMAN DOWNTOWN: And is also an idiomatic expression for a woman's—well, you know—

KING: Where do you learn such things!?

[*She rolls slowly onto her stomach and presses a button on the bedside table. The Mariachis are piped in.*]

WOMAN DOWNTOWN: Oh, let's say I was once the prisoner of a man who was hung up on that kind of language. I was forced to listen to those words over and over to—achieve his—erection. There's your Mariachis. What's the song?

KING [*hoarsely*]: —*Mujer.*

WOMAN DOWNTOWN: Just "Woman," huh?

KING: Yeah. Ain't that enough?

WOMAN DOWNTOWN: —Alone? —No. —Would you say so?

[*He rises, a hand unconsciously touching the fly of his pants.*]

KING: No. Alone is—

WOMAN DOWNTOWN: Sometimes lonely.

[*The phone rings. She springs up, catching her breath.*]

KING [*lifting the phone*]: *¿Juan? Sí, una noticia acerca del señor* Collister.

[*She makes an imploring gesture with her hands.*]

—Ah. —*Sí.*

[*He looks up at her.*]

—*Él está mejor.*

WOMAN DOWNTOWN: Out of danger?

KING: *¿Aparte de esto? ¿Seguro?* [*He turns to the Woman Downtown.*] They say yes.

WOMAN DOWNTOWN: When released?

KING: *¿Quándo está libre?* —*Muchas gracias, Chico. ¡Discreto! Ahora*—*los huevos rancheros, la señorita tiene hambre, ¡apúrate!*

[*He hangs up the phone.*]

En breve—soon—*cálmate.*

[*He rises again, but doesn't know what to do.*]

Listen. I will take you to the Judge. I can call a cab.

WOMAN DOWNTOWN: Don't you understand? It will always be the same cab, with the same driver, with the face of a demon. Like tonight. You must believe me. Please. *For your sake.*

KING: I could take a letter for you to him.

WOMAN DOWNTOWN: Not you. Rather your friend Juan—the one who calls me "classy papaya" . . .

[*She notes his troubled look and wants to distract him from her dilemma.*]

KING: You are gonna wrinkle that—elegant dress you got on . . .

WOMAN DOWNTOWN: I don't want to do that.

KING: Then would you—

WOMAN DOWNTOWN: —Like to remove it? Yes. My gift . . . from the General's wife . . . The skin of the Orientals is very delicate skin. She couldn't bear zippers on dresses, in fact she could wear only silk; she came of Mandarin, ancient Mandarin—lineage. She was utterly barbaric in her instincts, loved watching decapitations through binoculars from a mound of silk cushions in the cupola on the roof of the palace.

[*He has now slipped off her silk sheath and he looks down in humble awe at her delicate body in its silk lingerie.*]

I feel rather chilly. Do you?

KING: I got the, the elegant dress off you.

WOMAN DOWNTOWN: That must be why I noticed a change in the temperature of the room.

KING: —Do you enjoy a—good back-rub?

[*She laughs abruptly. There is a knock at the door.*]

WOMAN DOWNTOWN: The *huevos rancheros.*

KING: Should I tell 'em forget it?

WOMAN DOWNTOWN: We might be hungry—later.

KING [*reluctantly*]: —Yeah—yeah . . .

[*He crosses off. Inaudible voices come from the living room. After a few moments, King re-enters the bedroom, pushing a room service table on wheels—nervously.*]

They got tin covers over the—*huevos rancheros* and the plates are—hot . . . so no hurry . . .

WOMAN DOWNTOWN: We are all of us hurrying to the same place. So what's the hurry?

[*She stands still, smiling, trembling. He takes a faltering step toward her.*]

KING: —*¿Con permiso?*

WOMAN DOWNTOWN: —I do think you'd better!

[*He embraces her. She loses her breath and writhes involuntarily.*]

KING: *¡Por favor!* Hold still!

[*She breaks away from him. He is utterly baffled.*]

WOMAN DOWNTOWN: You—you—hu—hu—

KING: What are you trying to say?

WOMAN DOWNTOWN [*throwing her head back*]: *Human!*

KING: —Oh. —"Human." —Yes, I'm—

WOMAN DOWNTOWN [*with the same strange intensity*]: Human!

KING [*clasping her desperate head between his hands*]: You say "human" to me like something special about me. A living man is—

WOMAN DOWNTOWN: Yes! Human! To enter my life something human is special, this day, this night, this place, suddenly— you—*human! Here! What?* [*She gasps.*] I am back there, in-human. Behind estate walls of my husband's hacienda where I play hostess to Red Devil Battery Monsters. Great tall prison walls, guarded, oh, yes, private deputies guarded with revolvers the entrance; the gates had a guard house and were slid open and shut by electric-eye power, operated by power, and all the grounds were patrolled by—sports clothes for day and dinner jackets at night. —Guards guarded, they had such short friendly names, Pat, Bill, Ray and their, oh, their smiles at the gates and in the guardhouse and along the long drive, their smiles and their laughs and their shouts, it was not at all like the atmosphere of— San Quentin, but—I was—hostess to—monsters! —The guests were not—distinguishable from the guards; the guards were not—distinguishable from the guests. The guests and the guards shouted short names to each other with the same smiles, Hey, Pat, Bill, Ray, Hiyah, Hi, Hi, Hiyah. Credentials presented at the guardhouse, then the hell of the hollering. Come *awn* in here, Hi *ah* yuh, hi, hi *hiyah*, come in here, you folks drive right on in, and a dog pack, there was also a dog pack, and the dog pack all smiled too. It was all one big hell-hollering *death grin*. "Wanta drink now or afta you been to your guest house? Anything you want dial zero for service, you heah? Wonderful to see you lookin' so well; he-lllll! Ye-llllll." Oh, they trusted me to take their attaché cases with the payola and the secrets in code, and *why not? Wasn't I perfectly NOT human*, too?!

KING: *¡Cálmate!*

[*He rushes to catch hold of her. He lifts her and bears her to the bed and places her carefully on it.*]

¡Cálmate! You are out of that prison! *Cálmate.* Now be still, we're—human—together . . .

DIM OUT. MARIACHIS PLAY.

SCENE THREE

It is a while later in the penthouse bedroom. King and the Woman Downtown are both stretched out on the bed.

||||||||||||||||||||||||||||||||||||||||||||||||||||||||||||||||||||||||||||||||||||||||||||||||||||

KING: —Sleeping?

WOMAN DOWNTOWN: No, of course not.

KING: Tired out?

WOMAN DOWNTOWN: No.

KING: All those—cries . . .

WOMAN DOWNTOWN: I didn't hear any cries.

KING: I did. So I stopped.

WOMAN DOWNTOWN: Cries like something coming to life?

KING: I think you—exaggerate.

WOMAN DOWNTOWN: But I heard nothing at all. Just felt.

KING: What?

WOMAN DOWNTOWN: —Coming to life. [*Pause.*] —Afterwards, what do you do?

KING: What you want to do?

WOMAN DOWNTOWN: Rest. Beside you. I did a lot of talking before the—ecstatic outcries. Now you talk. Your turn.

KING: About what?

WOMAN DOWNTOWN: Your life, you—music . . .

KING: Yes . . . well. Mariachis. They gotta history to them goes back a long way. Before Maximilian—the Frenchman Napoleon sent us to be king. And in those days they played at marriages so they got them the French word *mariages* mispronounced to "mariachis." But then after Maximilian—we shot him!—and his wife Carlotta, she—

WOMAN DOWNTOWN: Went crying in the night through the palaces of Europe.

KING: Yeah. Well then they become just Mariachis that play in the streets and in cantinas. But we—we went a step better. We played in hotel lounges. Mainly I think because of La Niña.

WOMAN DOWNTOWN: Means little girl.

KING: My daughter was called La Niña. After she started work with us—you want to hear this? You're not just faking some interest?

WOMAN DOWNTOWN: I want to hear everything, please, please, I don't pretend.

[*He sits up.*]

KING [*sitting on the side of the bed*]: After La Niña started work with us, it wasn't just "King's Men," it was "King's Men with La Niña," and, honey, La Niña was so goddam terrific that after a month of singing with the vocal trio, she was singing solo *and she was dancing a flamenco better'n a gypsy fireball!*

[*The Mariachis fade in under his speech now.*]

In San Antone we played in The Ranchero Room of the big new hotel there, The Sheraton Lone Star, on the riverbank, y'know, in the heart of the city, and oh, man, they booked reservations for dinner five, six hours ahead or got no table. Outside that San Antone hotel, at the main entrance to it, La Niña's photo was blown up in color life-size; La Niña was the *Star!*

WOMAN DOWNTOWN [*stirring sensually so that her breasts are uncovered*]: I think she was just the daughter of the star. Tell me why you don't go back with King's Men and your Neen-ya. Tell me.

KING: Okay, I'll tell you straight. An accident—accident? Yeh, I guess you'd say "accident" of it. —This crazy accident happened—one week after we got a real name manager that was getting us gigs that would've made us hot as anything in the South. He said, "You start in The Hotel Reforma, the big one in Mexico City." "Man," I said, "oh, man, you got to be kidding—Reforma!!" —"Never tell me I'm kidding; it's not my profession to kid. I'm delivering the Reforma, to you, King. I'm booking you there for the summer, all of it; you can hold there all summer, and in the fall, well, on the roof of The Hotel Raleigh in Houston. Then, I think you ought to hit the Coast, at a spot like the Beverly Wilshire. Say, middle of November through the holidays."

[*He is suddenly boyish.*]

And he, my manager, he—he—criticized how I dressed; he said, "Look, dude, you're not an old dude!" —A wonderful thing to make a man believe. "Not old, and—*still*—appealing." —I thought, "Yes, older women." I said, "Yes, older women." —He said, "No, all women, because you are a big man with—"

[*Shyness makes him abruptly silent.*]

29

So I changed—outfits to suit him and—appeal to—

[*He stops, embarrassed.*]

WOMAN DOWNTOWN: Women.

KING: Yes. I did. And then—this goddam crazy thing happened. It happened that night at The Sheraton Lone Star in San Antone. We just finished a set and started to leave the bandstand, and I felt a stab in my head. I stumbled off the bandstand, fell on my face, blacked out. They broke some kinda capsule—

WOMAN DOWNTOWN: Oh, a popper . . .

KING: —Under my nose, but I—didn't get up. Well, they found this—accident—in my head.

WOMAN DOWNTOWN [*sitting up slowly*]: Found?

KING: A thing that happens to a man like that should have meaning, not be just an awful accident to *him*. Accidents don't have meaning. An yet, y'know most of the things that happen to people are accidents. You know that? Meaningless accidents? To them?

WOMAN DOWNTOWN: Yes, even birth and death, but love is not an accident.

KING: Ain't it? Are you sure?

[*She laughs richly, triumphantly.*]

Huh?

WOMAN DOWNTOWN: It seems more like . . . an Act of God to me . . .

[*She strokes his head; she abruptly catches a soft breath and leans over him.*]

KING: —I know. You just noticed the—scar.

WOMAN DOWNTOWN: And is that the accident that you were talking about? A scar from . . .

KING: Surgery, yes, a—surgical scar.

[*She rises from the bed. Her shock impels her to suddenly reach for a drink.*]

Thank you for a nice evening.

WOMAN DOWNTOWN: *What?*

KING: Have you got the time?

WOMAN DOWNTOWN: More time than a clock can hold, so don't think about it.

KING: I can't miss the last bus home. It wouldn't please my wife. And I got to please my wife because like you see, well, I am not working now. I am my wife, Perla's dependent, her—invalid dependent, and if I don't get home at night, she would hit the ceiling.

WOMAN DOWNTOWN: Good. It would knock her unconscious.

KING: Don't talk like that; she is a hard-working woman. Now I got a serious request to make of you. Don't drink no more in bed.

WOMAN DOWNTOWN: Don't deny me that comfort. I learned to do it to obliterate experience, but this night it's to hold it closer for a while.

KING: There's no future in it. No. I take that back, there *is* a future in it and it's a bitch of a future. Want to hear what a bitch of a future it is?

WOMAN DOWNTOWN: No, love, not tonight.

[*He grabs the drink from her hand.*]

KING: This much I will tell you. You drink in bed for experience and you'll wind up not a lady with some bad words in her head and some habits that don't fit a lady like, like screaming and clawing in bed. —How do I explain these marks you put on me, tell Perla I was in bed with a wild cat tonight?

WOMAN DOWNTOWN: No, with a she-wolf! —And no matter how I wind up in the future, still . . .

[*She extends her bare arms to him.*]

I would have known you, I would have lain with a king on a king-size bed.

[*Her arms extended, she grabs hold of him and draws him close again.*]

KING: —You know—

WOMAN DOWNTOWN: Yes, I know! I have known you!

KING: Love, lady, let go, I do, I do got to go, I—can't *not*—go—

WOMAN DOWNTOWN: You demand your release? Demand is granted! I relinquish you to the last bus home! And the lady that clocks you!

[*She cries this out as if she had been given a death sentence. He touches his head—shakes it.*]

KING: I think you got something in you that is wild like flamenco. You got something in you like my kid in Chicago—a heart on fire!

WOMAN DOWNTOWN: And you don't want to get burned in addition to getting those marks of the she-wolf on you? The episode is completed, not just for this night, but always? Or would it be heard in heaven if I offered a prayer that you'll be back tomorrow?

KING: I don't know about what is heard in heaven or not—but tell me, Miss Downtown Woman—what hotel are you in?

WOMAN DOWNTOWN: Answer my question first.

KING: I will be back tomorrow.

[*The Mariachis fade in, softly.*]

WOMAN DOWNTOWN: —Then the hotel I am in is the right one for the first time!

[*He stares at her from the door. Her eyes drop shut with a deep sigh of content and still he stands looking longingly back as—*]

THE ROOM DIMS OUT

The interior and exterior of a small frame house on the outskirts of the city. The exterior is the backyard. In it are two metal chairs. The interior contains a kitchen and sitting room area. It seems as if the house has drawn in upon itself for protection from the menacing profile of the city, and here is where a visual poetry must be present: sounds of the Wasteland, a wolf-call, calls. Perhaps we see figures watching, menacing. King is lighted as he walks slowly onto the set. He sits in one of the metal yard chairs. Across the Wasteland stand, in miniature silhouette, the towers of downtown Dallas. Perla is at the kitchen table, waiting up for King. She is a small woman, about King's age but appearing a good deal older. She is probably more attractive than she now seems to King—since his illness has made him dependent upon her. A disturbance in the Wasteland, accustomed as it is, makes her gasp and set the cup down with a crash. A primitive cry, much nearer, answers the explosion. Other cries answer. Perla rises and goes to the door.

PERLA: Stay back or I call police!

[There are more wolf calls, another distant explosion. King lights a cigarette in the yard. Perla crosses to the phone. King listens to the phone call. A ringing is heard persistently and another area of the stage is slowly lighted. La Niña is lighted, shivering in the chill of rising from love-making. McCabe is just visible.]

LA NIÑA: *Sí, Mama, ¿qué pasa?*

[Her voice is harsh and mocking. She is a girl of nineteen, but desperation has aged her and she is disheveled from "the bed." She continues, still harshly.]

34

—Well, Mama, have you hung up? —I didn't hear the phone click. —Are you still on the line? What a difference in you, this silence, not shouting at me!

PERLA [*slowly and fiercely*]: There are whores at the hotel where I work as housekeeper, but I do not talk to them except to say, "Can the maid come in to make up the bed now or is the man still with you?"

[*La Niña utters a wild flamenco cry of defiance. McCabe extends a hand toward her as if to restrain her.*]

I got to whisper or your father will hear. Or else I would scream at *you, ¡Puta!*

LA NIÑA [*abruptly soft*]: —Mama. How is he?

PERLA: What time is it in Chicago? In Dallas it's half past two. Ain't it that time in Chicago? Yes! A man answered the phone at half past two at night. Blood of Jesus, this life, these lies!

[*King has risen from the chair and listens just out of the interior light. McCabe is also listening in the opposite set.*]

LA NIÑA: Call him to the phone.

PERLA: He is not home.

KING [*advancing into the lighted interior*]: I am at home!

LA NIÑA: I hear his voice! King, King!

[*Perla makes a gesture of hanging up the phone.*]

KING: Call her back.

PERLA: —Who?

KING: La Niña. I heard her shouting my name.

PERLA: —King, you have dreams.

KING: Live on them, yes. She called me. Call her back. What is the number? I will call her myself.

PERLA: You think I was talking to her? Every two weeks a new address and a new—phone number . . .

KING: You lie.

PERLA: You dream.

KING: *¡Mierda!*

PERLA: You're sweating. Fever?

[*She touches his head. He strikes her hand away.*]

KING: You're always suggesting I'm still sick in the head, you *suci mentirosa!*

[*He jerks open the Frigidaire door and searches for beer. Both the Chicago and Dallas rooms remain lighted and neither scene freezes for the other.*]

KING [*throwing things out of the box*]: Too stingy to keep a beer in the Frigidaire?

[*Perla has thrust a can of beer she has just removed from a shelf at King.*]

Hot beer? *¡Muchas gracias!*

[*He tosses it into the corner. She picks it up and pours it over ice cubes. McCabe rises with a thwarted, anguished, choked sob. The light shifts to a poster of La Niña; her hand is on the poster and her imploring cry is heard.*]

LA NIÑA: King!

[*The poster should remain lighted through the hallucinatory duet with her father.*]

KING [*to Perla*]: In your purse this week was a envelope empty, empty envelope dated five days ago and from Chicago and it was not addressed here. Why? Huh? You got secrets from me about my daughter? A secret—correspondence between you and her that you don't want me to know?

PERLA: When she writes home she lies. I tell her to write me the truth, one woman to another. —Why did you look in my purse?

KING: *Because I steal from your purse! Sí, sí,* your purse is too tight so I take the price of two beers! Sometimes, excuse me, I take a little more to buy in a card game! Look, you want me to be like a beggar in front of the men at The Yellow Rose, not able to play a game of cards between sets there, not able to buy a beer and tip Charlie the barman?

PERLA [*shamed*]: What I have is yours . . . *Lo que tengo es tuyo, Dios sabe.* [*She presses her face to his shoulder.*] Oh, my God, I'm so tired.

KING: Then why don't you go to bed?

PERLA: —I smell perfume on you, a woman's perfume.

KING: Oh-ho, that. A drunk woman at the bar took out a spray bottle and—sprayed me. [*He is deceptively quiet.*] Be careful what you say to me.

PERLA: You don't want to go to bed with me because you got a woman downtown, I think.

KING: *Mierda.*

PERLA: I sit up for you nights, but when you come home you don't come in the house if the light is still on but you sit in the yard. Why? To look at the dump-heap, at Crestview-by-the-Dump-Heap in which we sunk our life savings? Till half an hour after I turn the light out? I say nothing, but I think, I feel, I'm a woman and I—love you.

KING: Things will work out soon. You're a brave woman. To-night? I got up on the bandstand with the men and I—*sang!* And there was applause almost like there was before. Soon I will send for La Niña and we will hit the road again. Remember her voice and mine together. *¿Los duetos?*

[*La Niña is lighted again, spectrally, downstage. He crosses to her and they sing together—a love song. The spot goes out and he returns to the kitchen.*]

PERLA: *Sí, recuerdo.* Love songs, between father and daughter. Not natural, not right. —Let's go to bed and—fight tomorrow.

KING: You go to bed, you get up early, need sleep. I want a cold beer.

PERLA: *¡Todas, todas las noches siempre lo mismo!* Go to bed alone.

KING: Yes, I'm no good.

[*Their eyes blaze at each other. Then he turns to snatch a beer. She turns away and walks wearily off. When she is out*

*of the light, he places the beer can back on the table. The
anger goes out of his eyes. He bends his head to sniff at his
shirt.*]

—Night—flight . . .

DIM OUT

ACT TWO

|||||||||||||||||||||||||||||||||||||||||||||||||||||||||||||||||||||||||||||||||||||||||||||||||||||||||||||||||||||||||||

|||||||||||||||||||||||||||||||||||||||||||||||||||||||||||||||||||||||||||||||||||||||||||||||||||||||||||||||||||||||||||

*A dull explosion at a great distance. Sounds of the Wasteland.
Cries. A clouded flare. Fade out as the Mariachi music is brought
up and the lounge is lighted. The Woman Downtown enters
that area slowly; she crosses to the bar. At the bar is a clutch of
conventioneers in a huddle, talking rapidly in low voices, all
wearing conical hats of red tin foil with the Red Devil insignia
on them. It is a month later. The Woman Downtown has a light
cape or stole about her shoulders, indicating a cooler season.*

|||||||||||||||||||||||||||||||||||||||||||||||||||||||||||||||||||||||||||||||||||||||||||||||||||||||||||||||||||||||||||

WOMAN DOWNTOWN: Mr. Barman, are you sure you haven't
received any word from Mr. Del Rey? He's half an hour later
than I expected.

CHARLIE: Maybe he's been delayed by family problems.

[*This interchange catches the attention of the conventioneers.
They come out of their huddle to stare up at the Woman
Downtown. Inadvertently, as she suddenly notices the insignia
on their caps, she gives a little gasping cry.*]

WOMAN DOWNTOWN: —Oh, Batteries, huh?

FIRST CONVENTIONEER [*grinning lasciviously*]: You wouldn't
be Mabel, would you?

SECOND CONVENTIONEER [*trying to stand*]: Is this Miss Mabel
Dickens?

WOMAN DOWNTOWN: —I'm sorry to—disappoint you, but I am

40

not "Mabel." Is the Red Devil Battery Company convening
here? I beg your pardon for interrupting your festivities. Battery
Red Devil! What cunning caps, I mean, cute like children's at
Halloween. Will all attending the battery convention allow me
to offer you—Mr. Barman, champagne for the gentlemen of the
Battery Convention and make sure it's imported. Battery men?
—Yes, *imported!* The best! And now please call Mr. Del Rey's
home; I have the number. Tell him to take a taxi. I'll meet him
at the entrance with the fare. But, if a woman answers—

CHARLIE: His wife, Perla?

WOMAN DOWNTOWN [*defiantly*]: Then just say that his men
are having a birthday party and the candles can't be lighted till
he gets here.

[*King enters the lighted area. The Mariachis go into a jubilant
ranchero to greet him. He turns to the Woman Downtown as
she crosses to him. She seizes his belt clasp and draws him to
her.*]

WOMAN DOWNTOWN [*in his ear*]: We're honored tonight by
the presence of a convention of Battery men; my husband's
closed in on me with—henchmen! —And you're an hour late!

KING: You're surrounded by me. I told you I'd be later because it was Perla's late work day, and supper would be later.

WOMAN DOWNTOWN: Supper, Perla come first and I wait for
a bus!??

MARIACHI: Come up and do a solo, King.

KING: No, no, *más tarde.* Perla can't understand that I come
downtown ev'ry night. She sniffs at my clothes when I come
home, sniffs them like a dog for you—perfume.

WOMAN DOWNTOWN: *Basta, basta, comprendo* . . . [*She drinks.*] Another, please. Have a beer.

[*He doesn't move. She crosses to the bar for the drinks and brings them to him. She hands him the beer can and it slips from his hand. He looks, troubled, at his empty hand for a moment, then shrugs with a wry grin and picks up the can.*]

KING: You don't drink down here, remember?

[*She surrenders the cocktail to him, and he empties it on the floor.*]

WOMAN DOWNTOWN: Yes, yes I—remember. Please, King, let's go upstairs. I have to talk to you. *¡URGENTE!*

[*His attention is abruptly diverted by the appearance of a swarthily handsome young man, slick-haired, cat-like, leaping onto a platform above the Mariachis and at once beginning a fierce, sexually aggressive crescendo on drums. King stares for a moment in frozen outrage. Then he crosses slowly, menacingly, to the stand. The Mariachis avert their faces, shamed.*]

KING: Julio!

[*The oldest Mariachi descends from the stand and places a hand—propitiatory—on King's shoulder. King strikes it away. His speech should be interspersed with Spanish expletives.*]

What is this? *Dios mío*, this *gato?* A drummer with Mariachis?

[*The small, grizzled-haired man spreads his arms wide in a gesture of helplessness.*]

Look! He stands shoving his *crotch* at—

JULIO: The manager insisted. *Yo no sé por qué.*

KING [*with desperate assertion of command*]: Management is *me!* Shit, I picked you all from little spick casinos; I build you to an outfit, King's Men, mine! Booked into Reforma, *México,* top-spot, Raleigh, Houston, Beverly-Wilshire, L. A.! Made, gave La Niña to star in East Ambassador Pump Room! And you spring on me a *maricón* in skin-tight satin pants, standing, jerking his crotch, and say to me "Management insist." *¡Escúchame! Management, me, insist OUT! Or am I OUT, have you counted me out now?*

[*The Woman Downtown holds him tight. He wrests himself free of her arms. At this point, King and Julio shout together: a scene of "presentation."*]

JULIO: Rey! King! We wait! But got to continue job here. Continue in Yellow Rose Lounge till you—

KING: I put you here.

JULIO: *Lo es.* But—

KING: What?

JULIO: We got to work till we know.

KING: Know what?

JULIO: If you come back or you don't; if La Niña comes back or not.

KING: Why do you ask if I come back with La Niña?

[*Julio shrugs, embarrassed. King turns downstage.*]

How can I keep control when I'm not active? Things slip out of my hand. Bring the manager here!

CHARLIE: He's—off!

[*King shouts to the Barman.*]

KING: *Charlie! Get me the desk!*

JULIO: King, why fight them now?

[*The Barman picks up the phone. King shoves Julio away from him, leaps onto the platform and hurls the Drummer off it. The Drummer lands nimbly on his feet with the smile of a cat, turns, and grins at the Woman Downtown.*]

KING [*to the Drummer*]: Git the fuck out of here, you *maricón!*

[*The Drummer goes off, laughing. The Woman Downtown draws King onto the stage apron.*]

WOMAN DOWNTOWN: No, now, love, you're sweating blood over nothing. He's gone. You threw him out and he's out! —May I request a number?

KING [*darkly*]: —Sí . . .

WOMAN DOWNTOWN: Julio! [*She calls to the Mariachis.*] "*Mujer*"!

[*They start immediately with the requested number. King is still breathing heavily. He moves a step and staggers, then grips her shoulders.*]

KING: —Yes . . . I   was—*ha!*—lost—balance . . . [*He   turns

downstage again to appeal his case.] They know it was—benign—
small growth, en-capsul–ated. . . . Just lifted right off the surface, like picking a—weed.

[*She kisses him. He turns to her.*]

No, no, wait till upstairs. *¡Hombres! Bésenme mucho para darme
suerte.*

[*King stares raptly; he rubs his eyes.*]

La Niña!

WOMAN DOWNTOWN: *¿Qué pasa?*

KING: Singing, dancing! No–a–vision . . .

[*He tries to laugh, then rubs his eyes.*]

WOMAN DOWNTOWN [*sobered with concern*]: Let's go upstairs.

KING: You go on up from the lobby. I'll take the back elevator.

[*The Woman Downtown crosses unsteadily out of the light.
The Mariachis are brought up. King crosses to them and shouts
over the music.*]

¡Muchachos! ¡Mañana! La Niña comes home. Kid's coming home
from Chicago! Tomorrow! How about that?

[*They respond with a jubilant "ranchero." King turns downstage and shouts.*]

Now we're living! *¡Hombres!* Sing it! La Niña tomorrow!

[*He turns to the Mariachis.*]

And today, this morning, I had my one-year check-up! The waiting period's over! Recovery is perfect! Doctor's sworn word today! Yeh, life is God, and good! —I'll see you all later . . .

[*The manager returns with the grinning Drummer.*]

GRIFFIN: *Julio!* —This drummer stays if you stay!

[*The Drummer springs nimbly onto the platform.*]

JULIO: King say no.

GRIFFIN: The president of the chain says *yes.*

JULIO: Why?

GRIFFIN [*contemptuously*]: You don't ask president why. You know why. Somebody's *money! Battery money. A lot!*

[*The Drummer begins; he builds to a crescendo as the forestage dims out. The crescendo continues through the set change, then halts abruptly.*]

SCENE TWO

The Penthouse bedroom of the Yellow Rose Hotel. The Woman Downtown enters with a vase of yellow roses. King is behind her as she enters the bedroom. He follows her, her eyes distant with brooding on the scene in the lounge.

||||||||||||||||||||||||||||||||||||||||||||||||||||||||||||||||||||||||||||||||||||||||||||||||||||||||||||||||||||

WOMAN DOWNTOWN [*to King*]: You're still furious. Why don't you leave it downstairs where it happened?

KING: It didn't happen to you.

WOMAN DOWNTOWN: What you feel, I feel. I know what you feel, and I feel it.

[*She laughs, then she loosens her shoulder strap.*]

KING: —Don't strip now. It makes you like a stripper in Vegas. D'you take me for a pick-up, a stud, after all the—what?

WOMAN DOWNTOWN: —*What?*

[*There is a shocked look between them.*]

KING: I got a cyclone in my head. You feel that, too?

WOMAN DOWNTOWN: I feel it blowing down walls.

KING: You, you—haul me up here and I might as well enter the room of a hotel hooker—no name, no past, no future, a smell of liquor on your breath and peppermint Chiclets to take it off or sweeten it for tongue-kissing and a spray bottle of—

WOMAN DOWNTOWN: *Vol de Nuit*, night flight from—

47

[*She cries out and throws herself onto the bed.*]

KING: Stay off the bed. Sit in the chair. Sit in it.

[*She crosses to the chair and stands helplessly by it.*]

Sit in it, Downtown Woman!

WOMAN DOWNTOWN: You never called me that.

KING: You called *yourself* that.

WOMAN DOWNTOWN: *You* never did till just now, and in an ugly way, too. King, please let tonight be lovely. There's a reason.

[*His look turns abstracted.*]

KING: —There is—no limit to time—but for us, there's a limit, a short one.

WOMAN DOWNTOWN [*springing up*]: I won't, I refuse to take part in this scene—you've drawn up in your confused head.

KING: "Confused head?" You never said that to me before. So this is a night for saying things the first time?

WOMAN DOWNTOWN: I meant only the disturbance downstairs!

KING: You said confused head!

WOMAN DOWNTOWN: *Who in hell on earth doesn't have a confused head now?*

[*The music of the Mariachis is heard, quadraphonic, distorted.*]

KING: I stumbled. The beer can slipped from my fingers.

WOMAN DOWNTOWN: What of it? I drop glasses, spill drinks, stumble, too.

KING: When drunk; I wasn't drunk. And you didn't even notice.

WOMAN DOWNTOWN: I told you I did, I noticed. Why, I've spent years, years noticing, seeming not but noticing, hearing or overhearing, sensing, suspecting, pretending to ignore with a constant well-practiced smile, but—always alert like a hunted thing in the woods, preparing to run, run—with a pack at my heels.

KING: You know how to talk. Stay off the bed and talk.

WOMAN DOWNTOWN: Suppose I have nothing to tell you I haven't told you in bed?

KING: Tell me what makes you a woman that can't give her name?

WOMAN DOWNTOWN: You're back to that.

KING: We never got to that. Just sit there like a lady and tell me, tell me who it is that I love and make love to.

WOMAN DOWNTOWN: You want me to give you the sort of factual information about me that you put down on hospital record sheets or immigration papers. A beautiful way to spend our last night together.

KING: Last night together's more bullshit. Tell me.

WOMAN DOWNTOWN: All right. Specifics. Till you cry hush.

49

Father's position? State senator. Mother? Died at my birth—oh, yes, I was told that often, accusingly, as if I'd *deliberately* killed her by being born. Birthplace? Hugh ranch in West Texas. . . . Isolated as madness. . . . You sing ranchero. Ever been on a big ranch? Heard these sounds at night?

[*She throws back her head and imitates a wolf howl, then the barking of ranch dogs.*]

KING: *Sí, sí, ¡ya basta!* Go on.

WOMAN DOWNTOWN: Wolves' howls, ranch dogs' answer.

KING: Go on without animal noises; I know them; I've known them inside of me and outside.

WOMAN DOWNTOWN [*flinging hands to her face and rocking with desperation*]: I don't have breath to go on!

[*King drops before her, clutching her knees.*]

KING: *Por favor*, for me—*necessario, querida!* The huge ranch—why?

WOMAN DOWNTOWN: Had to be huge to hold secrets.

KING: *¿Secretos? ¿Qué secretos?*

WOMAN DOWNTOWN: Of my father's Indian mistress, their ill-ill-legitimate child, my half-sister called Running Spring. Not a political asset to a statesman. The mistress hated me, spoke to me only in Apache. Apache was the language besides the wolves' and the dogs' howls nights! For me? A spinster tutor all in black like a widow spider, the black beads clinking!

[*She is clasping his clothes, the ranch becoming a vision in her.*]

Hard black eyes—critical, despising. —Lessons, I couldn't—learn from her. I learned English from leatherbound books in my father's library. Yes, it had to be huge, the ranch, to contain my loneliness, the nights, the wolf howls—the secrets . . .

[*She extends a rigid arm.*]

KING: What are you—?

WOMAN DOWNTOWN: Drink, please. Or let me stop now.

KING [*handing her a tumbler of water*]: *Aquí.*

WOMAN DOWNTOWN: Water is not a drink, love.

[*He presses it to her lips; she swallows. He clasps her tight in his arms.*]

The Indian child and I were equally lonely. We lived by a—dry spring in an *arroyo.* In late April or May it would fill with clear water and we would wade in it on opposite sides of the *arroyo,* sometimes—smiling shyly across it.

Thank you for holding me. It's not so hard to tell now.

At twelve I first menstruated and didn't know what it was, thought that I was afflicted with some unique disease that couldn't be mentioned—to whom? The black-bead-clinking tutor? I locked myself in room, wouldn't come out for my solitary meals. Father returned that day; he was told I'd locked myself up. —He sent me to a private school for disturbed children, more like an institution.

This confirmed my feeling that I was afflicted with a dreadful, shaming disease. I ran away, not back to the huge, night-howling ranch, but to my godfather, the Judge. His wife explained the curse to me, but the nights of the ranch were rooted in me too deep, they had made me—strange . . .

A girl that talked like a book and was full of secrets . . .

51

Problems followed problems; they do that, once they are started.

KING: Your father, he make no effort to get you back to—?

WOMAN DOWNTOWN: Hardly! —Absence ideal resolution of conflicts. —Empty water, fill wine . . .

[*Stunned, King tosses the water out of the tumbler and fills it with wine.*]

I never saw him again except on political newscasts.

KING: He disappeared from your life?

WOMAN DOWNTOWN: The dead do that. However—well, I belonged to society as the great southern statesman's daughter. —I was presented to society in the state and the national capital, too! Oh, what lavish balls, as if for a girl infatuated with splendor! —The walls of the tall, mirrored halls were covered with white flowers! I would enter the rooms and freeze as if standing on blocks of ice! —And my lips would form that icy, perfect smile for such occasions. Photographs show that I was a beautiful mask of—what I still don't know. You see, in me something was wrong, invisibly but incurably twisted by those desolate nights, the wolf-howling and the woman's cries of ecstasy which I thought were—anguish . . .

Now this will amaze you! I was acclaimed the most popular debutante of the season, and all of the parties smelt the same to me, like important state funerals which I'd had to attend!

All of a sudden, a breakdown, carefully covered up, no mention made of it. Partial recovery at—Institute for Re-birth.

Released, but not from the ice. Returned to the dazzling arena with no apparent shadow on the lifelike face. Dancing, I didn't feel a floor under my feet or the arms of my partner. Kept my eyes on glitter of chandeliers to keep from screaming, which worked; it worked somehow . . .

No, no, stay with your music, it's no goddam business of yours.

KING: Tell me everything, all.

WOMAN DOWNTOWN: Oh, I don't think I could stop myself now if I stood before a direct hot-line to the center of La Hacienda, which I possibly am! Barefoot little rice-paddie and cane-field people, innocent-eyed, simple-hearted as water oxen, asking just rice in a hand or a bowl out of a day's or a night's work—set to war with each other in spite of their blood connection, religious and culture connection, because, *because!* —You see, the huge, secret investments had to be protected by—sympathetically corrupt regimes . . . Oh, fighting Asia's like fighting God and time, but they figured they could do just that, no big hassle, you see, genocide for profits undeclared. —Well? —Doesn't it blow your mind? Well, doesn't it? You look incredulous. Why should you believe things before they happened? Well, I know before-hand; I can predict it exactly because I've seen it in blueprints drawn up at La Hacienda. No. I'm not the oracle of Delphi or Dallas, but I had *access* to those blueprints, the design for sur-rendering a democracy to rule by power conspiracy. —It did blow my mind, it broke through my numbness. Me, I'd elected, chosen my connection and finally my knowledge—

KING: —You were in this!

WOMAN DOWNTOWN: In it! Yes, I was in it, I was married to it, not just walking wounded but walking dead which made me adaptable to it! —Fool that wanted "specifics," well, you've got them. Yes, *amigo, amor,* I was in it, bought, they thought, for a beautifully trained front, accepting the bouquets and official greetings with a smile that looked almost real on the ramps of the privately owned jets. Oh, I was transported widely, world over, and, you know, it was a—hypnosis, the motion.

53

KING: And him? You were with him?

WOMAN DOWNTOWN: I've told you about his—obscene whispers while—

KING: —I think you're a little girl that's had a bad dream and run to papa's bed to tell him about it . . .

WOMAN DOWNTOWN: Just a—bad dream, huh?

KING: Well—I believe in bad dreams . . .

[*He unconsciously touches the now invisible scar on his head.*]

WOMAN DOWNTOWN: There now, no more about it. I never told you these things. Let's play never heard of, forgotten.

KING: Like the scar on my head.

WOMAN DOWNTOWN: Yes, and I, here with you, human, in Penthouse B for beautiful in my life, begun one month ago when you came in and locked the door behind you. —Well? Say something!

KING: I don't know how we're going to work this out but some way will—with locked doors, God, magic—anyhow for a while.

WOMAN DOWNTOWN: Only a while?

[*He looks up as if listening to something, a reverberation, an ominous thing, still not too close—beyond the room and the Woman Downtown—a thing that gives his words a meaning deeper than their surface: a distant, warning trumpet.*]

KING: Life is only a while. Love—longer.

[*The Woman Downtown smiles and caresses him.*]

Now, now, honey, leggo, I'm supposed to get home early tonight.

WOMAN DOWNTOWN: Whose supposition is that?

KING: You heard of Perla, my wife.

WOMAN DOWNTOWN: Not as much as your daughter, La Niña.

KING: This involves La Niña.

WOMAN DOWNTOWN [*sitting up*]: How?

KING: I didn't tell you? She's comin' home tomorrow for a visit. I won't be downtown tomorrow . . .

WOMAN DOWNTOWN: Neither will I, King. Not down this town, anyhow . . .

KING: She's only comin' home for a short visit before she goes back to work.

WOMAN DOWNTOWN [*pouring herself a drink*]: I didn't mean I was leaving because of her. Actually her visit is very well-timed, coincides with a trip I'm obliged to make. Your friend Juan in the kitchen, can he still be trusted?

KING: *¡Sí! Amigo. Amigo fiel. ¿Por qué?*

WOMAN DOWNTOWN: The Judge and I have been using him as go-between, a messenger service. Tonight under a metal cover from room service he sent me this letter. It's from the Judge. Read it.

KING [*reading with some difficulty*]: "Congress which other-wise would—would . . ."

55

WOMAN DOWNTOWN [*assisting him*]: "—adjourn—adjourn this weekend, will hold special session . . ."

KING: How do you know this is from the Judge? Not fake?

WOMAN DOWNTOWN: Juan has called him for me frequently. From a pay phone in town. Last night a manservant of the Judge got on Juan's bus and passed him this. —It's not fake. [*She reads.*] "You will accompany me. Reservation made on Braniff Airlines, Flight 68, departing for Washington, D. C., 5:00 p.m. My car will pass service entrance at 4:15 exactly . . ."

[*King looks up. There is a pause.*]

KING: When?

WOMAN DOWNTOWN: Tomorrow.

[*He looks at her darkly.*]

—Originals of those photostat papers I mentioned once—remember?—have been decoded. Judge Collister and I are taking them to the capital and I—if I shouldn't be able, after I testify, to return to here, or anywhere near here—would it mean I'd never see you again?

[*She sits down very gravely and searches his face with her eyes.*]

KING: This trip you're taking is—*peligroso—muy peligroso.*

WOMAN DOWNTOWN: Dangerous yes, very yes, very—

[*She continues to stare at him gravely. He takes the drink from her hand and drains it. He pours another and returns the*

56

tumbler to her. She drinks; he drinks again. Sounds are heard: fireworks crackling and horns blowing below.]

—Once you said, "Time has no limit for us."

KING: *Madre de Cristo*, forget it. The Judge is old, let him go! You? No.

WOMAN DOWNTOWN: No I'm going, it's an obligation, a, a—*my God, it sounds like all hell's broken out down there!*

[*She crosses abruptly to the window, raises the shade, then cries out repeatedly and wildly.*]

His sign, his sign, the Red Devil Battery sign, grinning at me through the window!

[*A red glare pulses in.*]

KING [*holding her*]: It's just an electric sign, honey. The building is being opened tonight by the Mayor. That's all, that's—

WOMAN DOWNTOWN: All? All? Battery Empire's devil-face grinning in at me?!

KING: Lie down, I'll—

[*He rushes to lower the shade.*]

WOMAN DOWNTOWN: *I can still see it; it pulses like blood through the shade!*

[*The red glare is extinguished. She crouches sobbing on the bed. He crosses to her. She plunges to him and starts tearing his clothes off.*]

KING: Now, now, love, you're—acting like a—

WOMAN DOWNTOWN: She-wolf? —Make love! Make love!

[*Pause.*]

KING: —After—all that?

[*She is undressing him. After a while she lets go of him and lies back on the pillows. He finally speaks huskily, shamed.*]

I'm sorry about that, but you know sometimes in a man it just don't work . . .

[*He sits on the edge of the bed.*]

—I want a cigarette.

WOMAN DOWNTOWN: I want a drink.

KING: Forget it. You don't need a drink.

[*They are both frustrated and angry.*]

WOMAN DOWNTOWN: I've got to have *something* tonight.

[*She reaches for the bottle.*]

KING: Put down the bottle.

[*She doesn't.*]

I don't like what you're doing; there's no future in it.

WOMAN DOWNTOWN: Just to wash down a pill, can't swallow it dry.

KING: You're going to wind up not young anymore, not beautiful, not elegant, but—

WOMAN DOWNTOWN: Yes, yes, *puta!*

KING: The kind that's picked up by any stranger and banged in alleys and back of trucks—I am—going to go home. How do I know what a wolf-howling woman might do or not do 'cause a—invalid man couldn't satisfy her one night out of a month.

[*Abruptly tender, she sits up, breasts exposed in the dim, aqueous light.*]

WOMAN DOWNTOWN: That was awful, forgive me! It made me vicious because I needed you so terribly this time that could be the last time.

KING: I guess a little of him was bound to rub off on you, love.

WOMAN DOWNTOWN: Moments, only moments. I turn to an animal.

[*Pause. He seems away.*]

—Am I with you or alone in space?

KING: —I think this Washington trip is—

WOMAN DOWNTOWN: I know what you think. You're right. Maybe just a gesture, and maybe—fatal. But doesn't it make a sort of dignified monument to mark where I was, a woman without a name, inclined to wolf-howls at night? Are you still on the bed?

[*He nods, silent.*]

59

Just seated beside me, not touching?

[*He slowly turns to look at her, then throws himself into her arms. The room is dimmed out. Music. When the room is lighted again, he is beside the bed, nearly dressed. She is watching him from the bed.*]

You know, there's somewhere beyond, and that time I think we went there.

KING: —Sleep, now?

WOMAN DOWNTOWN: Yes, now, quickly. This kind of exhaustion's a comfort, all the truth and then love.

[*He crosses to the window and opens the drapes.*]

Don't!

KING: I think it's daybreak.

[*He raises the shade to the pulsing red glare. She stares at it unblinking. He raises his right forearm and strikes it with his left palm.*]

Battery Man, here is to you, my salute!

WOMAN DOWNTOWN: Again, for me!

KING: Yeah, again, for us both!

THE SCENE DIMS OUT AND FAST CURTAIN

ACT THREE

||||||||||||||||||||||||||||||||||||||||||||||||||||||||||||||||||||||||||||||||||||||||||||||||||||||||||||||||||

||||||||||||||||||||||||||||||||||||||||||||||||||||||||||||||||||||||||||||||||||||||||||||||||||||||||||||||||||

We see the city in profile, many windows of tall buildings are catching the light of sunset; they are like myriad candles and they change color during the phone conversation, turning from gold to flame and to ashes of flame and, finally, to dark, with here and there a point of electric light or a touch of neon. On top of the highest tower is the only neon sign which is now visible. It is the Red Devil Battery Sign. It should not be consistently vivid; it should fade during episodes of the play from which it might distract. King is seated, naked to the waist, at a small kitchen table; beside him is a standing, revolving fan; his sweat-drenched shirt billows like a white signal of surrender before the fan which revolves with a low humming sound. Since King was last seen, he has suffered an accident: a gauze bandage about an inch and a half square, neatly secured by tape, makes it apparent that he has received an injury to his forehead. But what is most noticeable although not always present are odd hesitations and mistakes in his speech and inaccuracies in his reach for things. He may not be as mobile during the phone talk as the Woman Downtown, but he should remain by no means static. . . . As the scene begins there is a spot on the Woman Downtown, speaking in a voice strangulated by shock.

||||||||||||||||||||||||||||||||||||||||||||||||||||||||||||||||||||||||||||||||||||||||||||||||||||||||||||||||||

KING: Hello? Yes?

WOMAN DOWNTOWN: King! I'm calling from hotel kitchen; Juan is guarding the doors. Can't you speak? Am I Charlie the barman?

KING: No. . . . Perla meeting La Niña. At airport.

61

WOMAN DOWNTOWN: Had to call you even if they were there. King, King, they've killed him! They've killed him!

KING: *Cálmate, cálmate.* —Who? Killed?

WOMAN DOWNTOWN: Guardian! Judge Collister. Raided downtown office. Shot guards, entered and killed him. Looted the files, got decoded documents. But I'm . . . telling it backwards. King, I got this phone call today from some anonymous caller in the Battery Empire's legal department.

KING: The call a threat?

WOMAN DOWNTOWN: Yes, threat. Anonymous voice said: I speak for man from whom you stole documents. You make no move that's unknown. All is monitored. So be careful if you value your . . .

KING: Life?

WOMAN DOWNTOWN: Yes. Life. Voice continued: This eminent, unreachable, unimpeachable man has authorized us to advise you to leave country at once, leave continent. Go to Europe or Asia and stay there, passport and passage provided under false name, surrender all claim of connection as if you had never existed in his life or you won't exist in his life because you will *not exist!*

KING: I think they could do that with that much money, love, because that much money talks and when it talks there is no answer.

WOMAN DOWNTOWN: Oh, yes, it talks, money talks, not heads, not hearts, not tongues of prophets or angels, but money does, oh money hollers, love.

KING: —I think your master of Hacienda with his battery sign and his secrets has money enough and power enough to obliterate all life on earth, generals, rulers, presidents—and yours, Downtown Woman—

WOMAN DOWNTOWN: —King, what's wrong with your voice, you talk so slow and you—you—

KING [*looking slowly into space*]: —Something happened to me today—

WOMAN DOWNTOWN: *What?*

KING [*now speaking with a toneless deliberation again*]: —I started to walk to a store. All of a sudden I could see two sidewalks. I took the wrong one. [*He chuckles darkly.*] I came to in a—in a—drugstore with a cut on my forehead—

[*A door slamming is heard.*]

No, no, Charlie, no game of cards tonight.

[*Perla appears in her black straw hat with the plastic cherries.*]

WOMAN DOWNTOWN: Oh, I get it, they're home! Call me back in the bar!

KING: Yep. Maybe tomorrow.

[*King hangs up the phone. The Woman Downtown retreats into the shadow upstage.*]

PERLA: "Downtown Charlie" again, huh? Ev'ry time I, ev'ry night I—

KING: Where's the kid, Perla?

63

PERLA: They went to pick up some stuff for supper.

KING [*carefully, darkly*]: —They, did you say "they"? —She arrived with the Trio?

PERLA: —What's wrong with your forehead?

KING: That, nothing, a—little bump. I knew something was wrong. Is Niña married?

PERLA: What's wrong is that she *ain't*.

KING: She's—going—with—some man?

PERLA: Yeah, and the man is married.

KING: You just said she wasn't married.

PERLA [*shouting, shaking*]: I said *SHE* ain't, but *HE* is!

KING: Oh. Separate. No. Let me—get this—straight.

PERLA: Yeah, do that. Try! How did you get that bump?

KING: —Bump? Oh, nothing—important.

[*He grins at her savagely.*]

PERLA: Important enough to put a bandage on you big as that?

KING: We're talking on diff'rent subjects. Will you stick to one?

PERLA: Yes. The bandage.

[*She reaches to touch it, and he slaps her hand violently away.*]

AHH!

KING: That is not the subject. Will you take off that goddam hat with fake cherries on it? An' wipe the sweat off your face; you look like a spick chambermaid at The Yellow Rose Hotel with that shiny piece of straw like a chocolate sundae with cherries on it!

[*He snatches off the hat and rips it in two.*]

PERLA: *My hat!*

KING: *Donate it!* —To the *dump yard!* Now set down and draw a natural breath.

[*She snatches at a pencil and paper.*]

Don't snatch nothing from me! Remember I drove a car. A Mercedes limousine, before an accident made me your—*invalid— dependent!*

PERLA: —King . . .

[*She half-extends a hand to his head. He knocks it away.*]

KING: Yes, I lived like a king with King's Men and drove all night between gigs in a—limousine, not a trolley, before I became your—*invalid—dependent!*

PERLA [*suddenly in tears*]: —Your mother named you Rey. When you were a little boy they called you Reyecito, the little King.

KING: *Explícame*, La Niña, *¿dónde . . . ?*

PERLA: *Atiende, cállate.* She's been living almost a year with a married man in Chicago and—he's here! —Now are you satisfied with the explanation? Be prepared for a shock—she looks like a tramp!

KING: Cancelled? Out of her jobs?

PERLA: She ask me to go with her to the ladies' room at the airport. Soon's we got in, she grabbed my arm and said, "Mama, he's got a pistol on him!"

KING [*slowly*]: Looks like a tramp and is living with a—hood?

PERLA: *Shut up! They're coming in!*

[*La Niña enters the kitchen area, nervously meeting the cold scrutiny of her father. She is still beautiful but the fresh, young being which King remembers has been lost and he regards her as if she had criminally robbed him of it now as he faces his death. During the several beats of silence as they regard each other almost as if the scene were frozen into a tableau, we hear the ghostly Mariachis singing, just audibly.*]

KING [*finally*]: Well, kid?

LA NIÑA [*with a sobbing catch of breath*]: Hi, Daddy.

KING: I guess you were cancelled out. Makes two.

PERLA: What kind of way is that to receive your daughter?

LA NIÑA: —How did you hurt your—?

[*Perla gestures to La Niña to introduce McCabe.*]

Papa, this is Mr. Terrence McCabe.

[*There is another moment of silence. McCabe deposits groceries awkwardly, shuffles forward and extends a shaky hand to King.*]

MCCABE [*in a hollow, pleading voice*]: Hi, Pop.

KING: —Who the fuck is this man calling me "Pop"?

LA NIÑA: —Daddy, he's a—friend of—[*Her voice expires.*]

PERLA: He's the man that followed her down here . . .

LA NIÑA: We stayed outside; we thought you'd prepare him for—

KING: —Words—don't prepare—for appearance. Christ, you do look like a tramp.

[*McCabe circles La Niña into his arms. A great emotional violence rises in King.*]

Things have slipped from control! Money, Battery money!

LA NIÑA: King, what are you, what is he—?

PERLA: He hurt his head.

KING: *¡Cállate!* —The outfit, King's Men, is not managed by me. Now. . . . *Dig?* No more than you're in the Pump Room. *Why?* You put no value on nothing but fucking? Booze, you're on that, too? Booze and bed with—this prick?

MCCABE [*arm about La Niña*]: King she's shaking.

KING: Let her shake your hand off her!

[*He staggers to his feet and falls back into the chair, nearly throwing it over. McCabe catches the chair back.*]

—You prick of a mick come here with—unlicensed firearm and my daughter a slob!

[*King suddenly drops the pencil, jerks open the table drawer and pulls a carving knife out and points it at McCabe's groin. McCabe covers the threatened area with a hand.*]

Now we are both armed, but I have an advantage. My weapon's in my hand, ready for surgery on you if you don't surrender to me this unlicensed firearm right now.

LA NIÑA: King, we've got to work it out quietly, not this way.

MCCABE: Niña and me, we've been through a lot together; we can't explain all at once.

PERLA: King, King I think—

KING [*without looking at her*]: Think, do you, you think? I never thought you thought!

MCCABE: If we could all sit down without the knife pointed at me. Can't we? All? Sit down?

KING: Naw, naw, no room in the room, just, just standing room only! With La Niña singing!

[*He gulps a rasping breath. La Niña leans toward him, hands resting on the table, and sings.*]

LA NIÑA: . . . *Amor, amor, amor.*

[*His eyes focus on her slowly.*]

KING: —Yes, presenting—the star . . .

PERLA: Sing in the kitchen and put the food on plates; we can't have supper out of the boxes.

LA NIÑA [*breaking away*]: Who wants supper?

KING: *Supper?* They come for *supper?*

PERLA: Yes, it's time for—

KING: *Supper?*

PERLA: *¡Ayúdame en la cocina!*

[*She seizes the girl's arm again and draws her into the kitchenette, then returns for the bags. McCabe, assisting her, spills them. King sways forward.*]

MCCABE [*rushing to catch his shoulder*]: Watch it!

LA NIÑA [*in kitchenette*]: You never said a thing to me.

PERLA: I said wait till I call you.

LA NIÑA: Till *now*, for *this*, the *end?*

PERLA: *Here!*

[*Perla slams a plate on the table.*]

LA NIÑA: Supper off broken plates, Mama?

PERLA: Yeh, ain't everything broke?

[*There is a moment of silence. They turn opposite ways, sobbing. The Mariachis sing, offstage.*]

MARIACHIS [*offstage, softly*]: . . . *Amor, amor.*

[*There is another moment of silence. Then the phone rings on the table between the two men. King slowly picks up the receiver. Spotlight on the Woman Downtown.*]

KING [*speech slurred or gasping*]: Charlie? —Y'know I told you I can't come downtown tonight. My girl, my daughter's just come back from Chicago, with a serious problem—no game for tonight, cancelled.

[*King hangs up. The spot goes out on the Woman Downtown. Perla appears in the doorway.*]

PERLA: Downtown Charlie calling back so quick? —How stupid am I, King, in your opinion of me?

KING [*fiercely*]: Perla, give me time to think over this question.

PERLA: Oh, have I got some things to speak to you later.

[*She turns and leaves, beginning to cry.*]

MCCABE: Niña's been homesick, depressed since—she lost a—baby we were expecting . . .

KING: Expecting? A baby? By you? Baby face?

MCCABE: There was—no one but me.

KING: And your wife? Don't exist in the picture, not inside the frame of it? You're married but slept with my daughter and—!

[*He springs up and strikes McCabe. The blow is hard, but McCabe seems not to feel it.*]

—Did I hit you?

MCCABE [*quietly*]: Yeah. —Why not?

KING: —You rented a car. Get back in it and go.

MCCABE: Where? Without Niña. There's only two ways out. I stay with Niña or check out of my life.

KING: —Hysteria's for women. You've got a gun? —I have some trouble walking and I want to talk to you, private, in the yard. Help me. Don't make it noticeable to them. I'll hang on your arm like a—close buddy and we'll—make it slow . . . slow . . .

MCCABE: Yes, the talk should be private. Between us. —Ready? —*¿Pronto?*

KING: Wait till—I see better. [*He grasps McCabe's arm.*] All right. Ready. Start now.

[*Very slowly they advance toward the yard. The crossing is bizarre, the women watching in shocked silence. King and McCabe enter the kitchen. King tries desperately to move and speak naturally, but the walk and staring eyes betray his condition.*]

PERLA: *Hace frío afuera.*

[*She snatches up a shawl and puts it about him.*]

KING [*tearing it off*]: *For Christ's sake, bitch, don't put a mantilla on me!*

LA NIÑA: Papa!

KING: You know I got up with the men and I sang.

LA NIÑA: *Bueno*, Papa.

MCCABE: Take my jacket.

KING: Naw, naw, will you go in the goddam yard? It's cooler in the yard for—conversation that's—necessary.

MCCABE: There's two steps down.

KING: Yes, I remember the number.

MCCABE: Yes, it's cooler out. I feel a breeze.

KING: Yes—it's—cooler out. You feel—?

MCCABE: —A breeze. I've been sweating all day, very—profusely like I had a—fever. I guess—anxiety, Pop.

KING: —I have—limit of—vision. Chairs?

MCCABE: Yes, this way, no hurry.

KING: That's—your opinion, not—mine.

[*They advance downstage to the yard as formally as a pair of pallbearers.*]

I think—there is—a hurry.

MCCABE: Here they are. Take a seat.

[*Perla moves back into the house.*]

KING: Take your hands off me!

[*He falls, gasping, into one of the chairs. McCabe puts the shirt about him. He fastens one button and King tears the shirt open.*]

I will—not be—buttoned!

MCCABE: —I—understand. A man—

KING: Is not a man if—supported and limited and—buttoned. A Chinaman—said to me once—in next bed at—hospital—"Death is not big enough to hold life and life is not big enough to hold death"—and yet that morning the problem—solved itself very simple with a white canvas curtain to—

MCCABE: —Conceal the—?

KING: *Solution!* Your name is?

MCCABE: My name's—Terry McCabe.

KING: Sorry I . . . forgot. Such a nice Irish name. You run out of potatoes too fucking quick and you come here too many and you decided it wasn't potatoes you wanted but liquor and parades and wakes and political power. Bosses and corruption. Oh, back home you're into revolution but here you're into— ripoff. . . . Christ, you babyface mother! —My head aches. Go in. Go in the bathroom and get me—

MCCABE: What?

KING: Something begins with a "D" they use to give me for killing the head pain—Demerol! —Don't say nothing about it, just bring it out.

MCCABE: Right. [*He crosses to the house interior.*] Excuse me. Where is the bathroom?

[*La Niña points.*]

LA NIÑA: Mama, you are lying. *¡Mama, estás mintiendo!* There had to be signs first, something you noticed!

[*Perla is both guilty and defiant.*]

Stop messing with delicatessen stuff.

PERLA: I worked, didn't I work?

LA NIÑA: Never till he fell!

PERLA: You think it was not work for me, too, the travel, the packing, and I got no applause for it, nobody shouted me bravo, nobody called me *olé!* But when—

LA NIÑA: Yes, now you are admitting it now.

PERLA: I tell you like it was, yes!

LA NIÑA: Not facing me with your eyes, but—

[*She seizes a carton of salad and hurls it at her mother. Perla turns on her with a blaze of fury.*]

PERLA: Now with eyes I face you! Signs, there were signs. While I worked, he worked a crossword puzzle, and when I came home to make supper, he still worked on the puzzle, and at supper the fork would slip from his fingers and he would look at nothing like he saw something in nothing!

[*McCabe reappears in the doorway.*]

LA NIÑA: But you never, never did you call me except to say,

"Stay in Chicago," and to make sure that I stayed and to call me
"*Puta!*"

PERLA: It was not you but me that my husband belongs to, I
thought, I believed, till he come home with perfume-of-women
smell on him and sat out there in the yard chair till I went sleep-
less to bed, all hell out there exploding like in my heart! While
the warning, the signals begun to grow.

LA NIÑA: —Mama, I think it's too late to fight over what's left
of him.

PERLA: You got something in your hand.

MCCABE: Just—

PERLA: *What?*

MCCABE: Something he asked for from the medicine cabinet.

[*Automatically he reaches out for La Niña and draws her to
him. In the yard, King stands facing the house, fists clenched.*]

I like him, I respect him, I bring him what he needs for his pain.
Oh, the beer, the six-pack . . .

[*He picks it up and goes into the yard.*]

KING [*as McCabe crosses to him*]: *Dos Gatos* . . . two cats.

MCCABE: I got the, here's the— [*He hands King the Demerol
bottle.*] —and beer.

KING: Open for me. —Shit, not the beer, the—

MCCABE [*very gently*]: Sorry, yes. [*He gives King a capsule.*]

75

KING: Now to wash down the—

[*McCabe extends the beer can to him, but King seems not to see it. Very gently, McCabe thrusts the capsule in King's mouth and then lifts the opened can to his lips.*]

—yes, turning to—dummy, situated by—dump heap . . .

[*There is an explosion in the Hollow. King shouts toward it as if a last cry of defiance. McCabe assists him into the chair.*]

Now. Tell me how did it happen.

MCCABE: I could tell you better if you dropped the knife from your hand, Pop.

KING: One lie out of your mouth and it goes in you, "Son!" So it stays in hand!

MCCABE: My life before I met Niña was—*vacant* as that . . . vacant . . .

[*He gestures toward the Wasteland.*]

KING: —Dump heap?

MCCABE: Yes, empty, empty. Emptiness filled with violence! Oh, I tried to occupy, to satisfy myself with statistics . . .

KING: Occupy with stat? Lift your goddam crybaby head and speak plain to me! *¡Chico!*

MCCABE: Statistics on buyer-consumption—response to—promotion—commercials.

KING: Don't know what you're—

76

MCCABE: *I said that I'm a trained, well-trained, computer is what I said! Programmed to be not human! But—I am! Human!*

[*Perla throws open the door.*]

KING: Don't—shout at—my head—"Son!" —There is a *pressure*—in it.

MCCABE: You said "speak plain." [*He rises abruptly.*] What more do you want to know? I went out nights alone. Sat alone at bars. Then once—the room where Nina, to this place on the lakefront, where she worked with a trio. I saw what was *not empty*. Stayed and stayed till they shut the place each night. Finally one night at closing I worked up the courage to send a note to her: "Let me buy you a drink, please."

KING: She answered this—*proposition?*

MCCABE: Don't—don't call it that!

KING: Then call it *what?*

MCCABE: —It was no proposition. It was an—appeal. She granted. I could talk, just held her arm close against me. And we didn't talk at the table. Very little, very difficult till—

KING: What?

MCCABE: My eyes blurred—over with—

KING: *¡Lágrimas! Tears!*

MCCABE: I seemed to be looking at her through—tears. Then she took hold of my hand. And what she said to me then was: "—You—are in pain like—my father." Then— "Wait here a

77

moment." —She—booked a room and came back and said, "I will hold you tonight, I will just hold you," she said.

KING: "Hold you?" That was all?

MCCABE: *Then.* But the next night—*all* . . .

[*A distant explosion is heard.*]

What was . . . ?

KING: Shots between gangs in the Hollow. —Between here and downtown is this hollow for dumping. Fog collects in it. It is—playground for—kids, yeah, they dig caves in that hollow out there in that—rubble, heaving rocks at each other, some nights, shots, explosions, soft drink bottles with nitro. Oh, it's not—not—put in headlines but—is going on all the time and people don't dare admit—how far it has—gone, no, not yet, but soon it will blast too big for—city—denies. I'm expected downtown.

[*He is standing, gripping McCabe's shoulder for support.*]

MCCABE: I will drive you there, King.

KING: Not downtown, just—is she watching? List'ning?

MCCABE: No.

KING: What are you? Baby-face *boy* or *man?*

MCCABE: La Niña is pregnant, again.

[*King stares at him silently for a moment; then drops the knife.*]

KING: Now. Give—firearm.

78

MCCABE: That—subject we'd—covered.

KING: Not cover till firearm surrender. Give me the . . .

MCCABE: If you say "stay." I can't until you say "stay."

KING [*shouting*]: *STAY*. My child bearing your child?

MCCABE [*urgently, with love*]: My child growing in yours.
Life is continued that way, a child of a man bears a child of a
man—

KING: And the man—dies.

MCCABE: But the life of him is continued.

[*Another explosion is heard in the Hollow.*]

KING: I taste—blood in my—mouth . . .

[*He staggers; McCabe holds him tight again.*]

Gracias. Yes. Stay. But then, what? For La Niña? To turn to a
slob, gradual, like her *madre*, not singing but remembering singing? Too tired to dance flamenco, but remembering flamenco?
This girl I made and gave to the world, she what could have
stood higher than the new sign on the new skyscraper, tallest in
Corona, one you see nights miles away. *That!* —That—height—
for her was my dream, the dream of a man with quick death in
his skull, this flowerpot of a skull with a flower in it that is
cracking the pot. I think you want just your comfort, not her—
glory.

MCCABE: No—no.

KING: Aw, don't say no, just "no" like a kid asked if he stole
something. No is too easy to say to a question that big.

MCCABE: I want her to be again the way that she was—the way you remember and I give you my word.

KING: —When a man gives his word he gives a—guarantee of it, a pledge, a thing for, for security on his word, if he's a stranger. And you're still a stranger to me.

MCCABE: What do you want?

KING: I want the—firearm you got on you.

MCCABE: Here. Take it. It's yours. I have no use for it now. She will deliver the child and she will go back to what she was made for, by you. I want her to be the—

KING: —Highest?

MCCABE: The girl I first knew—

[*He has surrendered his revolver to King.*]

I may be a stranger to you. You're not to me.

KING: Just tell me which way is the gate because I'm leaving now. I have a date with a downtown woman, downtown.

MCCABE: Let me take you there to her.

KING: No, no, just where's the gate.

MCCABE: Let me walk you to it.

KING: I told you I want no more assistance. I just wanted your word and the pledge in my pocket. I see it now, I'll make it.

[*He stumbles rapidly forward but encounters the fence, not*

the gate, and crashes fiercely through it. He stands by the
broken fence as King's Men appear at either side of the stage.
McCabe clings to the back of a yard chair for a moment. His
eyes are tightly shut, then he looks into the sky. There is a
muted clash in the Hollow.]

MCCABE [whirling toward the house]: Niña! Niña!

[Perla rushes to the kitchen door; she makes a disgusted gesture and turns to the girl.]

PERLA: ¡Tu caballero loco te llama afuera!

[La Niña descends into the yard. McCabe extends his arms
to her.]

MCCABE: It is settled between us.

LA NIÑA: How?

MCCABE: I stay! —He wants it.

LA NIÑA: Where is King?

[Perla approaches behind them. The following dialogue is fast
with some overlaps.]

PERLA: Supper is set if anybody wants food.

LA NIÑA [clinging to McCabe]: Where is the pistol?

MCCABE: He made me surrender it to him for permission to
stay.

PERLA [hearing this, crying out]: You surrender death to
him! King!

MCCABE: A King can die like a king.

PERLA: *Where is he? Look! The fence is broken!*

MCCABE: That is a man's right if he wants it.

PERLA [*rushing to the broken fence*]: A crowd is on corner. *King!*

[*She collapses to her knees, clinging to the fence post. The house and yard begin to dim. McCabe catches hold of La Niña as she rushes toward the fence.*]

MCCABE: Stay here, be calm, think just of our child in your body; for King and for me, keep it safe in you . . . safe.

THE YARD DIMS OUT COMPLETELY

SCENE TWO

The Mariachis sing as a section of the lounge is lighted. There is a spot on the Woman Downtown.

||||||||||||||||||||||||||||||||||||||||||||||||||||||||||||||||||||||||||||||||||||||||||||||||||||||||||||

DRUMMER: *¿Qué tal, Chiquita?*

WOMAN DOWNTOWN [*fiercely*]: Intimate form of address like to *puta*. Translates to "How'm I doing." *Bueno, muy bueno,* like the best in hell ever.

[*The Drummer, giving a quick look about, circles her low with an arm.*]

Your hand is presumptuous, Drummer, I'm still in King's kingdom.

DRUMMER: King's lost his kingdom.

WOMAN DOWNTOWN: *¡Disputable!*

DRUMMER: *Por favor.*

[*He circles her unsteady body again.*]

WOMAN DOWNTOWN: Snake arm, quick as rattler from desert rock.

[*The bar phone rings. King appears on the forestage, opposite side.*]

Phone!

[*The Barman touches the phone to establish it. The profile of*

83

the city is dimly visible between King and the Woman Downtown. The Woman speaks furiously to the Barman.]

He's hung up! You took so long to call me, he's hung up!

KING: No, love, I—try to—spe—I am—trying to—speak.

WOMAN DOWNTOWN: I can hear you breathing.

KING: Yeh. Still breathing. I started to come downtown but only got to the drugstore on the corner.

WOMAN DOWNTOWN [*controlled*]: That's all right. I'll come there in a cab. Barman, call me a cab, quick. See, I've called a cab. Now give me the address. I will come and get you.

KING: No, just listen. I called to tell you good-bye.

WOMAN DOWNTOWN: Hold on a minute. Barman, have this call traced. Have a phone operator trace where it's from, please hurry, it's—emergency! [*She has covered the mouth of the phone.*]

KING: I heard you, there's no time.

WOMAN DOWNTOWN: Oh, yes, there is, there's always more time than you think. And listen, you great son of a bitch, you owe it to me. Give it to me or I'll—

KING: Yes, I know what you'll do and I can't stop you.

WOMAN DOWNTOWN [*turning from him to cry out to the Barman*]: Have you traced it, have you got the address—drugstore—Crestview.

[*The Mariachis fade in.*]

King? Love? It's all right, you know. King. King, I've moved
to a room with no Red Devil grinning through the window, a
room the opposite from it but with a bed king-size for you to lie
with me once more and I've prepared the room for you. I knew
you were coming downtown. There are—roses, fresh linen, clean
air! Mariachi. I will undress you. I'll hold you.

[*She is crossing the stage, imploringly, toward him.*]

Now, just give me the address of the drugstore to bring you
where we can go together as it's meant to be, King. Listen. Do
you remember the night I first saw you? My life began that
night and is going to end this one. Can you hear me, King? All
I hear is your breath. Tonight I won't say a word that isn't right
for a lady to say, I swear. We have to go but we have to go
together.

KING: Honey, I told you—I can't make it downtown.

WOMAN DOWNTOWN: Oh, but you can and you will.

KING: —Good-bye, love. I think the drugstoreman has called
an ambulance to take me away and they'd drill through my
skull to cut at the flower, to prune it. What would be left? A—
imbecile?! No! I have to go quick, now.

WOMAN DOWNTOWN: I dare you to hang up on me, don't you
dare hang up on me. I will stop the ambulance at the drugstore.
I'll take you to my room at the Yellow Rose or be—an uniden-
tified—female body—mutilated past recognition back of a truck
in an alley if you don't tell me where—

KING: Good—bye—love . . . *much* . . . *loved!*

[*He staggers to his knees and in the fall the revolver slides
out of his reach. The Pharmacist, an elderly man, gentle, anx-
ious, stoops to pick it up.*]

85

That's—mine, return, please.

OLD MAN: *Son,* they're coming for you. Hang on, just—hang on . . .

[*King tries to rise; the Old Man helps him into a chair but stands back as King reaches for the revolver now in the man's jacket pocket.*]

KING: Christ, it's all I got left, Pop. She said she is coming.

[*The Drummer is in whispered colloquy with Charlie. As the Woman Downtown staggers, near collapse, back to the bar, Charlie, face impassive as stone, jerks his head toward the shadowy upstage, a signal to the Drummer who exits that way.*]

WOMAN DOWNTOWN [*to the Barman*]: Traced it, did you trace it?

CHARLIE: Wasn't time.

[*She turns about frantically and sees Crewcut at the entrance.*]

WOMAN DOWNTOWN: Get "Crewcut" away from that door. I'm coming out that door, and it's worth this and this and this and this to me to get to the taxi rank on the curb!

[*She has thrust bills across the bar.*]

CHARLIE: Know the way?

WOMAN DOWNTOWN: Will find it if not obstructed.

[*There is a vertiginous swirl of color on the cyclorama as she*

*sways, extends her arms sideways for balance, staggers for-
ward. Crewcut calls to Charlie.*]

CREWCUT: Where's she going?

CHARLIE: To the Drummer Boy in the alley. Don't follow; the
Drummer can handle this better alone out there.

[*As the bar dims out, the dark menacing towers of the night
city appear, projected on the cyclorama. In a very dim circle
of light the Drummer is seen, waiting. A door slams and the
Woman Downtown enters the dim light.*]

WOMAN DOWNTOWN: Drummer!

DRUMMER: *Sí, tamborilero* that King don't like but you do.

WOMAN DOWNTOWN: *Cab, cab!*

[*The Drummer seizes her and pulls her out of the light. He
pulls open her coat, touches her brutally, roughs her up. He
takes a picture; the light of a flash-photo is seen. The Woman
Downtown scratches the Drummer's face.*]

Cab, cab!

[*The Woman Downtown breaks free and exits. The Drummer
puts a handkerchief to his face. As the Woman Downtown
exits, calling for a cab, Charlie and Crewcut re-enter.*]

CAB DRIVER [*offstage*]: Okay, lady, no screamin' is necessary!

CREWCUT [*entering*]: You let her go loose, you goddam—

DRUMMER: Clawed my face bloody!

CHARLIE: Follow! Crestview Pharmacy. Move!

[*The Drummer—watched by Charlie and Crewcut—runs off-stage after the Woman Downtown.*]

CROSS FADE LIGHTS

SCENE THREE

The pharmacy section of the stage is lighted.

KING [*to the Old Man*]: She—said she is coming. Old Man, Pop, don't move. I go to lock door against all that could come to attend—this necessary finish but the lady—nameless—with eyes I want to look into—a last time . . .

[*He stumbles forward slowly, revolver in hand. The Woman Downtown, disheveled, dress torn, appears before him. Slowly, she lifts her hand, meaning "Wait!"*]

WOMAN DOWNTOWN: Wait!

KING [*hoarse, tender*]: You did find without address. Should have stayed where we live, but—

WOMAN DOWNTOWN: I never lived there with anyone but you.

KING: Here—is dangerous—for you. Outside on corner they gather, the—gangs from—

OLD MAN: *Lady, call police. I know those voices out there, bombers, young hoods from the Hollow!*

[*Four apparitional Mariachis appear and advance in their silver-embossed black velvet suits and wide sombreros.*]

KING [*going into fantasy, attempting to stand straight and salute*]: *¡HOMBRES!* [*He smiles reassuringly at the Woman Downtown.*] Now you are—protected! —By my men.

WOMAN DOWNTOWN: King, there's no one but you and me and the Old Man.

[*In a formal, dance-like fashion, his visionary Mariachis divide about King and the Woman Downtown to form a line between them and the Old Man crouched near the wings, downstage left. The Old Man's quavering voice keeps up a continuous, barely heard, threnody of despair.*]

OLD MAN: Can't sell out, but got to quit.

KING: —Love—request number.

OLD MAN: Got to leave . . .

WOMAN DOWNTOWN: King, oh, King, you're dreaming!

OLD MAN: Got to close . . .

KING: *Sí, sueño.* Dreams necessary.

OLD MAN: Gangs raid houses, stores . . .

KING: "Life is—too big for death?" [*He shakes his head with a savage grin.*] No! *Al contrario.*

OLD MAN: Police don't come . . .

KING: *Solicita el número.*

WOMAN DOWNTOWN: Can't—think! Please! We knew it was coming! Our last time but not here, *¡por favor, no aquí!*

OLD MAN: Don't even pray for help now . . . [*He kneels, covering his face.*]

KING [*oblivious, almost exalted*]: *La señorita solicita una canción, un vals, hombres.*

[*They play softly. King speaks to the Woman Downtown.*]

Don't move. Look me in the eyes.

WOMAN DOWNTOWN: You? Too?

[*He nods. They take opposite chairs, their eyes fixed intensely on each other. Pause.*]

KING: I love—a lady.

WOMAN DOWNTOWN: King, do you respect me, now?

KING: —You? Respect? —Yes! *¡La verdad!* Truth. I give you that name, now.

WOMAN DOWNTOWN [*in a last anguished appeal*]: Then come downtown with me now?

KING: Hospital called, ambulance coming. No time.

WOMAN DOWNTOWN: A cab, my new room are waiting; believe me, I know the best way.

KING: —Your clothes are torn?

WOMAN DOWNTOWN: Just that?

KING: Keep looking in eyes.

[*He lifts the revolver slightly toward his head. She gasps and half rises.*]

Don't move.

[*The door is forced open with a crash and the Drummer*

91

enters. He flashes a photo. King blinks, then speaks, articulating slowly, fiercely.]

—Oh. Drummer! You—got acquaintance!

[*The revolver has swung toward the Drummer.*]

WOMAN DOWNTOWN: Yes, he followed me.

DRUMMER [*retreating, cat-like*]: If you fire, you hit her, not me.

KING: No, not her! [*He staggers rapidly forward, thrusting her back into the chair.*] I see narrow but straight. First, tell me who pays you, employed by, for what?

[*The Drummer makes a sudden dash for the door. As he flings it open, King fires. The Drummer falls. The Woman Downtown screams. King crashes to the floor with the Woman Downtown clinging to him. The pharmacy door hangs open and a fantastic group enters. These are the wild young denizens of the Hollow. They seem to explode from a dream—and the scene with them. The play stylistically makes its final break with realism. This break must be accomplished as if predetermined in the* mise en scene *from the beginning, as if naturally led up to, startlingly but credibly. The kids, adolescents, some pre-adolescents—they could be as few as four or as many as seven—are outlaws in appearance and dress. The Hollow marks them with streaks of dirt on their faces, bloodied bandages, scant and makeshift garments. Among gangs of this kind there is always an individual who stands out, not as leader with such warring factions, but as the most powerful, the pre-eminent one. In this case, one older than the others, totally fearless, a boy-man with a sense of command and an intelligence that isn't morally nihilistic. His speech is almost more like gutteral explosions of sound with gestures. At the entrance of the gang members, the Old Man has rushed to his cash box and thrown himself despairingly across it. A couple of kids, screeching like monkeys, rush at him, but the dominant youth shouts a gutteral command to them. This dominant one has on his singlet, crudely red-lettered, the word, "WOLF"—significantly not "WOLVES."*]

WOLF: *Ahgah, nada! Leddum lone wid is nigguls!*

[*Something in his harsh voice rouses the Woman Downtown from her crouched moaning position over King's dead body. Wolf's eyes are on her face, demented with grief. Her eyes meet Wolf's. Her head is thrown back, teeth exposed as a she-wolf snarling. A moment passes. The Wolf nods and advances to her, lifts her to her feet; she offers no resistance. In his supporting hold, she recognizes or senses something rightly appointed as her final fate.*]

WOMAN DOWNTOWN: Yes, you. Take me. Away . . .

[*A savage little hood rushes at her to tear the watch-bracelet from her wrist. Wolf strikes the kid aside and awkwardly but strongly encircles the Woman Downtown's waist with his wire-torn arm.*]

WOLF [*beyond dispute*]: She goes wid us. This is—

WOMAN DOWNTOWN: Woman. [*Gasp.*] Down. [*Gasp.*] Town . . .

WOLF: It's enough, for me and for all. Listen! This woman. Ya mother.

BOY [*with a touch of challenge*]: Motha of—

WOLF: Yes. Mother of all.

BOY: Why?

WOLF: Because she is Sister of Wolf!

[*A flare goes off behind them and a muted sound of explosion is heard in the Hollow. Against its lingering, warning glow, the denizens of the Hollow all advance, eyes wide, looking out at us who have failed or betrayed them. The Woman Downtown advances furthest to where King's body has fallen. She throws back her head and utters the lost but defiant outcry of the she-wolf. The cry is awesome. There is a second explosion and a greater, whiter flare, exposing more desolation. Wolf takes her hand. All are standing motionless.*]

THE SCENE DIMS OUT

THE END

New Directions Paperbooks—A Partial Listing

For complete listing request free catalog from
New Directons, 80 Eighth Avenue, New York 10011   † Bilingual

For complete listing request free catalog from
New Directons, 80 Eighth Avenue, New York 10011   † Bilingual